CLEO LA RUE
MARCH 8, 1995
NEW BRUNSWICK NJ

H

The Dilemma of Modern Belief

OTHER BOOKS BY SAMUEL H. MILLER

Prayers for Daily Use
The Great Realities
The Life of the Church
The Life of the Soul

THE DILEMMA OF MODERN BELIEF

The Lyman Beecher Lectures, Yale Divinity School

by SAMUEL H. MILLER

Harper & Row, Publishers
New York, Evanston, and London

FOR MOLLY

Contents

(vii)

Preface

Lest someone plunge into the following pages with the expectation that he will quickly find new methods or exciting solutions to the problem of preaching in the twentieth century, a word of warning should be raised. For many years I have known both the joy and embarrassment of preaching, but when the invitation to deliver the Beecher Lectures came, I found myself confronted with a serious doubt that preaching as such could be dealt with very radically or even meaningfully until one faced a much deeper issue. Such was the climate of the contemporary mind, the conditions under which the assumptions and implications of a Christian epoch had changed so thoroughly under the impact of a technological culture, that one had to ask how religion itself, or faith, could be construed or identified before one asked about the requirements of pulpit method and presentation.

It was for this reason that I tried to discern some of the salient marks of the religious climate, or perhaps I should say more accurately, the religious implications of the present world in which religion finds itself uncomfortable or even somewhat unintelligible.

Preaching which assumes that proclamation is all that is necessary, disregarding the nature of contemporary consciousness, I think is too facile and too arrogant to commend itself as more than an ecclesiastical presumption. The work of God continues in the mind and heart of modern man, and until we respect with honesty and perceptiveness the changes that are wrought there, we shall walk the treadmill of old clichés. The answers required of us simply cannot be stolen from our ancestors.

As I have said elsewhere, "The ancient dogmas no longer dominate the imagination; the modern divisions no longer capture man's loyalties. The shape of life has changed; the patterns of truth are different; the questions have new terms; doubts have deeper dimensions; the hunger of the heart and mind has been enlarged; the risks have greater costs. . . . The church cannot amuse itself with the posture of past prestige or present popularity; it has inherited a revolution. It will be judged by the measure of its action in dealing with the radical changes in our world, not by its nostalgic reverence or its sterile respectability."

The generosity and hospitable warmth of the members of the Faculty of Divinity at Yale, particularly of Dean Liston Pope in his invitation and of Acting Dean Forman during my stay, deepened a debt to Yale which has many ramifications. To Mrs. Florine Blanco, my secretary, who saw my patched and scribbled manuscript to final intelligibility amid many other tasks, to Mrs. Bunn Thompson, who straightened out the more tortured of my phrases, and to Paul and Lois Chapman for their preparation of the index, I wish to express my earnest appreciation.

Samuel H. Miller

Cambridge, Massachusetts

The Dilemma of Modern Belief

(1) The Double Meaning of Secularity

For a long time we have been trying to understand our age. Over the last one hundred years the term "modernity" has been something of an obsession with philosophers, historians, preachers, reformers, essayists, and a host of others. We have tried to weigh its essential worth, analyze its components, detect its direction, identify its values, mark its shape and substance. It has been many things to many men. For Karl Marx it was the millennial age of the proletariat; for Spengler, the twilight of civilization; for Whitman, the age of the common man; for Henry Adams, a dismal fate. For Nietzsche it was decadent and yet the door to new possibilities; for Dostoevsky it was dangerously demonic; for Bury, the age of liberty; for T. S. Eliot, a wasteland; for Ortega, the upward rise of the barbarian; for Kafka, a nightmare; for Auden, the age of anxiety. For politicians it was the age of democracy; for scientists, of space travel and unprecedented power, and for artists a new loneliness and a deeper exile.

Choose as you will—optimists, pessimists, hopeful or dismayed
—the extremes are all present and at least to some degree justified.
The age was extravagant both in its achievements and in its evil.
Hopes were never higher, nor dashed quite so low. Ambition was
unlimited, but catastrophe was almost universal. Power increased
by leaps and bounds in every sphere. Disease and suffering were
magnificently lessened, yet no age had seen such fiendish cruelty
or deliberate barbarism.

If we have had our difficulty in deciding what the age was really
like, it is not strange. Its man-made wonders were spectacular;
yet so were man's crimes. If we handled nature like giants, we
handled ourselves like idiots. Our time took in such contradictions
that it was almost impossible to compose anything like a synoptic
vision of it. It is hard to live in any age and see it at the same
time, but the landscape of our era was particularly large and
mixed. Across it floated all the dreams and illusions that blotted
out or blurred the harsh reality of it. We lacked distance, for we
were caught up in it and swept along by it, and yet we could not
altogether forswear the effort to see it steadily and see it whole,
to weigh it and have a word for it.

THE SHIFT TO A NATURAL WORLD

In his autobiography, André Gide tells of an experience he had
as a young boy. He had reared a caterpillar and was keeping the
chrysalis carefully in a small, narrow uncovered box in which it
lay like a mummy in its sarcophagus. He writes:

I used to examine it every day, but never perceived the slightest
change, and I should perhaps have despaired of it had it not been
for the little convulsive movements this semblance of a creature
made when I tickled his abdomen with the nib of my pen. It was
really alive then! Now on that day as Monsieur Tabourel was cor-
recting my sums, my eyes fell on the box. O Proteus! What did I
see? Wings! Great green and pink wings beginning to stir and quiver!
    Overwhelmed with admiration, with joy, dancing with enthusi-
asm, I could not help seizing for want of a better divinity, old

Tabourel's fat paw. "Oh, Monsieur Tabourel! Look! Oh, if I had only known . . ."

I stopped short just in time for what I had been meaning to say was, "If I had only known that while you were explaining those deadly sums, one of the mysteries of life, so great a one, so long expected, was going on at my elbow!" . . . A resurrection like Lazarus's! A metamorphosis, a miracle. I had never yet beheld . . .

Monsieur Tabourel was a man of education; calmly but with a shade of astonishment or blame or something disapproving in his voice:

"What," said he; "didn't you know that a chrysalis is the envelope of a butterfly? Every butterfly you see has come out of a chrysalis. It's perfectly natural."

At that I dropped Monsieur Tabourel's hand. Yes, indeed, I knew my *natural* history as well, perhaps better than he. . . . But because it was natural, could he not see it was marvelous? Poor creature! From that day I took a dislike to him and a loathing to his lessons.[1]

Here in this episode stands a simple text which might well sustain a long and elaborate exegesis of the passage from a religious world to a natural one. The grace that always surprises, the miracle rising from the commonplace, the leaping joy and recognition of divinity, all move quickly and sadly into the hard bitterness of sophistication which declares with finality, "It's perfectly natural."

Indeed, everything had suddenly become perfectly natural. Surprises of any sort, anywhere, were eyed with suspicion, waylaid, delayed, and finally prepared for and controlled; the miracles that rose from routine were pushed back into the dull chrysalis and analyzed to find out where they began and how they developed, slowly and understandably; the leap of joy and the reach for divinity were moderated by discipline to lie in wait and observe with cunning, until there was no question of divinity at all and the data were every whit clean of any ulterior or ultimate factors. Everything—man included—was perfectly natural.

[1] André Gide, *If It Die,* Dorothy Bussy, trans. (New York: Modern Library, 1935), p. 83.

Or we may take a more serious episode in the sixteenth century, the place Marburg.

The disputants are two powerful theologian reformers: Martin Luther and Ulrich Zwingli . . . The dispute is about the eucharist. . . . The bread and the wine—are they the body and blood of Christ, or are they "mere" symbols? . . . Luther, with all his deviations from the traditional dogma, is the man of the Middle Ages. The word and the sign are for him not merely "pictures of thought," but the thing itself. Yet for Zwingli, steeped in the enlightened thought of the Italian Renaissance, this is a barbarous absurdity. The sacrament is "merely" a symbol, that is, it symbolically represents what in itself it is not.

This is indeed a very particular occasion. . . . Never before had this question raised so much dust and generated so much heat. For now it is merely the theological climax of a deep revolution in the thoughts and feelings with which men respond to the world they inhabit; the Miltonian opportunity for a "Truth who, when she gets a free and willing hand, opens herself faster than the pace of method and discourse can overtake her." There will be a world which must find it more and more difficult even to grasp, let alone accept, what was in Luther's mind when he fought Zwingli's "demythologising" (an activity as hazardous as the word that expresses it, tongue-twister for angels and bedevilling the minds of men). Lost will be that unity of word and deed, of picture and thing, of the bread and the glorified body. Body will become merely body, and symbol merely symbol. And as for the refreshing wine, it will be drunk by thirsty souls only when in the very depths of their thirst they are quite sure that it was pressed from real grapes in the mechanic way.

What, then, is the nature of the revolution signalled by a theological dispute that seems concerned merely with degrees of symbolic "literalness"? . . . Zwingli's argument did to the status of religion, poetry, and art what some time later Copernicus did to the status of the earth. . . . at the end of the period that we rather vaguely call the Middle Ages there occurred a radical change in man's idea of reality, in that complex fabric of unconsciously-held convictions about what is real and what is not. . . . And ever since Zwingli the most common response to the reality of symbols has been a shrugging of shoulders, or an edified raising of eyes and brows, or an apologia for poetry, or an aesthetic theory.[2]

Time would fail me were I to pick up the innumerable events, biographical and historical, which illustrate this passage of man from one world to another. His stance and perspective, his method of operation and his attitude, all have changed, subtly, silently, and for the most part unconsciously. But now, looking back, we can see the change in direction, the fork in the road. We are in a new world, and so deep in it we cannot get out of it. There is no turning back.

THE CHANGING CLIMATE

The secular age has come. On all sides it proclaims itself frankly, proudly, even a bit boisterously. The state has unshackled itself from the dominance of religion; science has long since liberated itself violently from any concerns of faith (or even morals!); art fears the debilitating touch of the church as the very touch of death; industry goes its merry way of marketing, advertising, manufacturing, without regard to religious scruples, hoping only not to offend at too great a cost. None of the basic concerns of man's spirit any longer carry more than a most attenuated relationship to religion. The world operates very well in most areas without paying any attention at all to religion. In fact, faith has been put into a pocket, to which the world may revert at odd times when and if it pleases. It is no longer a consistent or pervasive element of our life.

Accompanied by many shrill cries of coming doom, the secular age has risen about us like a tidal wave. Few institutions have escaped the flood. Most of society's traditional attitudes have changed; the stance of mankind has shifted, and everywhere the ancient apostrophe to the gods has been replaced by a singular

[2] Erich Heller, *The Hazard of Modern Poetry* (Cambridge, Eng.: Bowes & Bowes, 1953), pp. 11 f., 13.

confidence in the world candidly and realistically viewed. Sentiment, we assume, simply obscures the truth; faith is a distracting anachronism; dreams and scruples alike are a hindrance to a clear view of reality.

Certainly every aspect of the religious spirit has lost its intensity. Prayer is no longer the first resort in an emergency but the last, after all the scientific possibilities have been exhausted. The sacred has evaporated from all but the most intimate and numinous of experiences. The fear of the bomb is more intense than the fear of God. Conversion and redemption have been replaced by education and adjustment. The church itself has become acculturated, confirming the established mores of respectability rather than raising the question of man's inadequacy in the light of God's eternal judgment.

Thus the climate of our world has changed. In one sense it has not happened suddenly. There have been many premonitions, many prophets. The sensitive reaction of genius might well have warned us, had we not been so blind and so dull. The gathering accumulation of subtle shadings, the tiny tremors that grew to thunder, all made themselves known to the few.

The responsible origins of secularization are often confused with the more immediate causes. There is no doubt that the objective habit of science, the routine character of industry, the mechanistic influence of the machine, have all heavily encouraged the increasing secularity of the West, but there are deeper sources than these, of greater import. Both the Hebraic realism of the Old Testament and the Greek development of science entered very early into the heritage of our culture and set up certain determining directions and attitudes that have finally culminated in our present condition.

And yet even now, with so much evidence at hand, multitudes will not believe that anything radical has happened. There are changes, to be sure, but there are always changes. Men have different ideas of things, but they are still men. What is, always has been and always will be. Here and there, however, a man's eyes will be opened and a vision of what has been hidden will be suddenly granted him. What he has seen a thousand times and yet has never really seen, he will suddenly know. The world has changed.

As Osbert Sitwell describes it:

> It is difficult to know the end of the world when you reach it, as difficult as to sound the depths of Hell's all-consuming fires, illimitable and unconfined. There are no signposts to tell you where you are. The sky is still there, the light shines down, from heights canopied or azure. In the shapes of the clouds, in their groupings and shiftings, you can still read visions of fortune as easily as of disaster. You think in the same way. Moreover, there is the cruel physical, or animal, persistence. You sleep and eat—eat with the same movements of jaws and hands. Nothing comparable to the collapse of the West, which we are witnessing, has happened since the fall of Constantinople to the Turks: and even then, the shock was not so great, because the inhabitants of the great maritime city, though for so long masters of the world, had not called in Science to give them an assurance of infallibility; they too, however, those of them who survived to see the next day, were by habit and necessity compelled to eat and sleep, and in time to work.[3]

But this has happened now on a large scale and at profound depths. A new way of looking at life, and therefore a new way of living and understanding things, has developed. The sky is the same, and the sun; the rain falls, and the earth rolls on from season to season, and all is the same—or almost. Something is missing, forgotten perhaps, or simply dropped out of existence. At any rate, we cannot make the same sense out of things; they do not add up to the same sum as when we were little, or when Dante dreamed or Kant philosophized. We put them all together, but something comes out of it that never before appeared. We cannot make the same poems with the stars, or the same science with the

[3] Osbert Sitwell, "Laughter in the Next Room," *Atlantic Monthly,* Volume 182, Number 4 (October, 1948), p. 83.

sun, or the same wisdom with thinking, or the same morals with conscience, or the same religion with faith. It is very much like playing chess with all the old counters, knight and king and pawn, but with strange new rules that have never been used before this minute. Perplexing! And desperately upsetting—especially if one is strictly honest about it.

The world has been stripped down to what Nietzsche called its "ipsissimosity," down to the "object," the "thing." The pageantry of myth and holy day, of poetry and ritual, has been swept away with a brusque, businesslike gesture, leaving all days alike, dulled down to a bitter frenzy of routine. The great metaphors have drooped and died; the prose of speech has grown lean and hard, dispensing with syntax and taking on the staccato chatter of a machine gun or the flat-footed factualism of an inventory. Art has turned its back on classic forms given in creation and fantasied with its own erratic improvisations, picking up the ragtag ends of dreams and states of mind.

Nature is no longer religious, either in its pagan vitalities or in its Christian miracles. It is simply natural. Work is no longer surrounded by the ritualism of religious import; the songs and dances have dropped away, leaving the sheer drudgery of it plain to sight. War is no longer attended by symbolism or a call to the gods; it is now a straightforward business, with no plumes or costumes, no ceremonies or heroism, no courtesies or rules. Holidays are no longer holy, decked out with color and grand parades, sacred processions and riotous gaiety; the multitudes now rush from the great cities like lice from a dead body, scrambling in a vast headlong exodus to the mountains or the sea, where all holy days are alike, merely a chance to "get away from it all."

In man's life everything has been denuded of its religious quality. Birth, puberty, marriage, sin, death—once the pivotal points of spiritual significance, have now lost their sacramental depth. Everything has become natural, biological, social, and quite clinical.

There are no distances, no depths, no essential mysteries. Everything is on the surface, from which data can be easily skimmed off.

GLORY TURNED TO GLAMOR

Advertising has become the religious expression of such secularity. If manufacturing is intent on producing more things, then things must be justified, given value, their glory (or glamor—the name for superficial glory) revealed. The advertiser becomes the poet in our culture. In his imagination the product becomes the most desirable thing on earth, filled with extraordinary fascination, potent with a magic capable of transforming drabness and dullness to ecstatic heights of success. If such a gadget can be possessed by any means, by painful denials and endless installments, then all the harrowing frustration of being just one more human being lost in the anonymous mass is transcended. One shines, one stands out, one is important, one is gazed at enviously, one has been saved. A brand of tobacco makes a wisp of a fellow feel like a dauntless he-man, a kind of whiskey becomes the stamp of explorers and daredevils; a face cream turns an ugly duckling into a princess in one application; a detergent properly used resolves all the drudgery and nasty housewifely duties into a paradise of uninterrupted bliss. Salvation was never more ardently proffered by the church in its most fervent evangelism to save the world than it is now by frenetically hepped-up hucksters, who promise the full delight of heaven to those who are bored in their chrome-plated hell, by giving them more of the same sort of thing.

Three things tend to characterize the nature of this secularity. There is no unity, no superstition, and no easy peace for man. To be sure, none of these over-all conditions is absolute, but in terms of relative emphasis they indicate some of the more or less obvious conditions of the culture that has developed in Western civilization during the last three centuries.

THE LOSS OF UNITY

Unity was lost in the mounting secularity that erupted with the exhaustion of medieval culture and the rise of the Renaissance. As R. G. Collingwood points out in his *Speculum Mentis,* the consciousness of man underwent a radical differentiation by which the various component parts of his psyche broke loose, so to speak, and moved into an independent freedom, each in its own right. The aesthetic sense was no longer dominated by religious themes; the political sense likewise threw off religious constraints; discursive reason developed science and repudiated any authority but truth considered objectively. This development within man was quickly manifested in the exterior world by autonomous vocations and self-conscious activities in the realm of art, government, and science. Each sphere stood in rebellion against the religious unity that had traditionally bound them together. Church and state were now carefully set apart; the artist and the saint went their separate ways, developing a high degree of suspicion of each other; and the scientist and the ecclesiastic began a long battle of endless controversies. After three or four centuries of such development, both within man's consciousness and in his cultural activity, we now stand at the point where we are unable to identify, for the most part, the religious factors in the political sphere of government; nor are we able to express our religious experience in the aesthetic mode of visual symbols or myths; nor do we know how to recover the religious implications of a scientifically objectified nature. We are split, schizophrenically divided, holding within ourselves and our world several competing—perhaps contradictory—exclusively inclined fragments, each boisterously claiming to be the whole, or at least the highest.

This loss of unity is nowhere more evident than in the recent descent of philosophy from its classic position of seeking to see life steadily and whole, of affirming the coherence of all things and identifying, however variously, the comprehensive principle or factor which made for understanding. Today philosophy has turned its back on speculative efforts, on metaphysics, on any imaginative probe toward the shape or symbol of meaning in things, and rests content in logic—largely the syntactical logic of language. How microscopic this may become is hard to say; that it represents a symptom of atomization, of a world no longer strong enough to strive for a vision of unity or even to concern itself with the possibility that there may be one, is significant indeed. Secularity is the loss of unity both in the consciousness of man and equally in the culture derived from his sensibility.

SUPERSTITION AND MYSTERY

A second characteristic of secularity is its lack of superstition. This, to be sure, is only relatively true, for with the repudiation of many traditional religious superstitions, man's credulity remains a fertile ground for unsupportable illusions in new fields, such as politics and science. Our age has been replete with fantastic beliefs which have corrupted the sanity of modern man, turning contemporary politics into a nightmare and otherwise sober research into utopian fantasy.

Basically, however, the revolution of thought which Bacon introduced as empirical science has slowly but surely brought about a disciplined sanity of mind at every level of human experience. We have learned to be honest, to observe objectively, to describe accurately—in short, to check our fears, our projections, our exaggerations. We have now achieved a matter-of-factness, a habit of truthfulness, a desire for unvarnished, unembroidered reality We have tried to find out what is out there, not to dress it up or put words in its mouth, or make it over into something we like better. All in all, we have acquired a new asceticism of the mind. We will not lie for nature; we are trying to make truth more dependable.

Now, to be sure, if we have eradicated superstition from wide reaches of thought and life, we have also, to an equal extent, removed mystery. Our exactitude has been accomplished by focusing our questions more and more on clearly answerable phenomena.

We have isolated each unit from everything around it, from the whole which supported it and gave it meaning. We have cut it off from the depth of why it existed at all, and from the infinite consequences it entailed because it existed. We settled for knowledge that could be useful because it was dependable and repetitive, and let go of everything that could not be measured, analyzed, predicted. To be literal seemed so much more truthful than to be comprehensive. Knowledge of fact seemed to promise more than the wisdom of meaning. We preferred the small change of hard currency to the larger value of symbolic paper money.

A secular world has no time for mystery except in detective tales of a constantly changing frontier which moves at the thrust of the scientist's experimental finger. It moves quickly to self-assurance in all realms from the strictly scientific to the subtly theological. In science the basic and unalterable dimension of mystery as the primary character of existence tends to be reformulated as merely the unknown, which is pushed back by expanding knowledge, while in religion its loss is manifested in the reduction of worship to an ecclesiastical entertainment unattended by awe or contrition.

In every area the symptom of the loss of mystery is indicated by the rise of techniques—techniques of control, of manipulation, of short cuts, of speed, of mass propaganda. Technique is a method that reduces the mystery of any reality being dealt with in order to handle it quickly. Indeed, civilization develops by this method, slowly but surely complicating itself until the actions of men are perforce increasingly channeled into routines or habits. This method is marked by the evaporation of freshness or immediacy. In science it develops into technical research, a fertile ground for clever mechanics devising gadgets and gimmicks; in religion it gives rise to a particular kind of ecclesiastical secularity by which all the institutional elements of faith can be manipulated with virtuosity and apparent effectiveness without the slightest reference to religion itself.

Or, again, the loss of mystery is indicated by the disappearance of the category of miracle from religious thinking. "Miracle," however gross, irrational, or superstitious in its appearance, is at bottom the sign of mystery, of that which transcends man's ability completely to comprehend or exhaustively to know any event or thing. The miracle may be thought of naïvely or superstitiously as the erratic interjection of God's finger into the routine of nature, but beyond that level it still represents the larger reality of anything that cannot be adequately explained in the simple process of cause and effect. The loss of this depth of mystery, this dimension of transcendence, is essentially the mark of secularity.

ALIENATION AND INDEPENDENCE

The third mark of secularity is found in the alienation of man. When the world loses its unity, man simply does not know where or what he is; when the world loses its dimension of mystery, its more-than-factual character, man is no longer able to see himself reflected in the world in which he originated. He suffers alienation on both counts. He is born to make some sense out of the confusion of history; therefore to live in a time of chaos, of jostling claims and contradictory purposes, is to be more than uncomfortable. He is affronted, baffled, pushed away, and feels himself "outside." He is, moreover, born to wonder, to perceive intentions, far-off shadows of hope or fear, intimations of destiny, perspectives beyond time or memory, and such being his condition he looks upon a literal world as strange and not his own. He does not belong to it. Something absurd is born out of this disparity. Something was born in him, thrives in him, something elusive but ineluctable, ineradicable, which cannot rest content with the naked skeleton of matter-of-fact.

It was Hegel who first used the word "alienation" to describe man's predicament. Since then, Kierkegaard, Dostoevski, Nietzsche, and the proliferating school of existentialists, psychiatrists, and novelists have been unable to do without it. It represents an abnormal condition induced by cultural changes and now assuming the proportions of a collective neurosis.

The name used generally to describe the type of human consciousness that derives from alienation is "rebel." Our recent history, someone has said, resembles nothing more than a series of "rebellions." Our literature is crowded with these figures that fascinate and horrify us—Raskolnikov, Ahab, Brand, Meursault.

There is, however, a profound and passionately positive aspect to alienation. It is independence, a virtue highly esteemed and much praised in the history of our own land and widely in the modern era since the Renaissance. We have celebrated in literature and morals the individual sufficiently bold to stand out against tradition, the mass of his fellows, the protection of society. We have elevated the kind of hero who stands alone, fearlessly defies authority, and wins his victory singlehanded. If secularity releases a man to a lonely alienation vis-à-vis nature and history, it also creates in him a sense of independence which enlarges his freedom and comprises in itself a destiny of considerable enhancement of the human venture.

It is thus that the double meaning of secularity makes itself known. Unity is lost and with it the coherent pattern of meaning it sustains, yet the loss is characterized by a tremendous burst of energy expressed in the diverse forms of cultural activity in art, science, government, and religion. Superstition is swept clean with the coming of secularity, yet with the loss of superstition there also goes the mystery by which existence is deepened and reality in its total aspect respected. Finally, the impact on man himself is indicated by the fact that he becomes independent, achieves a notable freedom, fulfills his individuality, and yet at the same time feels himself alienated, an outsider, alone in a world to which he does not belong. Secularity thus has double meanings and is in itself not a solution to the religious problem. It is in essence only the restatement of the problem.

THE WORLD "COME OF AGE"

This becomes significant in the light of more or less recent statements by Dietrich Bonhoeffer about the *Mündigkeit,* or coming of age, of our world. Generally, in the preaching of Protestantism, secularity has been roundly condemned as an outright evil. Expanding secularization of the world was taken to be the same as de-Christianization. The more secular we became, the farther we departed from Christianity. Secularization was taken to be the mark of the devil in our time. In characteristic revivalist simplicity the world was lost, its ways were the ways of sin, and nothing good could come of it. This still remains the burden of most of the preaching done in Protestantism. Such preaching completely misses the point. Bonhoeffer's basic demand is that we cease this all too easy bifurcation of reality. There is no way to conceive of God or Christ without the world. Let him speak for himself.

The division of the total reality into a sacred and a profane sphere, a Christian and a secular sphere, creates the possibility of existence in a single one of these spheres, a spiritual existence which has no part in secular existence, and a secular existence which can claim autonomy for itself and can exercise this right of autonomy in its dealings with the spiritual sphere. The monk and the nineteenth-century Protestant secularist typify these two possibilities. The whole of medieval history is centered upon the theme of the predominance of the spiritual over the secular sphere, the predominance of the *regnum gratiae* over the *regnum naturae;* and the modern age is characterized by an ever increasing independence of the secular in its relations with the spiritual. So long as Christ and the world are conceived as two opposing and mutually repellent spheres, man will be left in the following dilemma: he abandons reality as a whole and places himself in one or the other of the two spheres. He seeks Christ without the world, or he seeks the world without Christ. In either case he is deceiving himself. Or else he tries to stand in both spaces at once and thereby becomes the man of eternal conflict, the kind of man who emerged in the period after the Reformation and who has repeatedly set himself up as representing the only form of Christian existence which is in accord with reality. . . .

There are not two spheres, but only the one sphere of the realization of Christ, in which the reality of God and of the world, which has been accomplished in Christ, is repeated, or, more exactly, is realized, ever afresh in the life of men. And yet what is Christian is not identical with what is of the world. The natural is not identical with the supernatural or the revelational with the rational. But between the two there is in each case a unity which derives solely from the reality of Christ, that is to say solely from faith in this ultimate reality. This unity is seen in the way in which the secular and the Christian elements prevent one another from assuming any kind of status independence in their mutual relations.[4]

It is in this world that modern man has become mature and stands in a new relation to religion and to life. His adulthood, his independence, his clear-eyed objectivity, his tenacious hunger for truth, his unrelenting search for reality, all these things must be respected as the very ground of his being as a religious person. He cannot reach his destiny by simply disregarding the world. Its secularity is precisely his religious realm. In it and with it he must find what men in other days called salvation.

The world today is stripped down, absolved of all supernatural alliances, scrubbed clean of special events divinely arranged, deprived of the *deus ex machina,* the undeniable proof, the outright arrogance of miracle. Yet it is God's creation; He made it. The fact that we are no longer children or adolescents, propped up and sustained in our credulity by such assertions of direct invasion, or of immediate and implacably authoritative acts of the divine, means that we have entered a new stage of religion. Our faith now must be in a God not seen directly; a God whose acts are not separable from existence itself; a God in whom we must have faith, not be-

---

[4] Dietrich Bonhoeffer, *Ethics,* Eberhard Bethge, ed., Neville H. Smith, trans. (New York: The Macmillan Company, 1955), pp. 63–65.

cause we have been overwhelmed by direct epiphanies, but because His glory pervades the common structure of things.

Wallace Stevens expresses the character of the modern world in its search when he says:

> We keep coming back and coming back
> To the real: to the hotel instead of the hymns
> That fall upon it out of the wind. We seek
> The poem of pure reality . . . We seek
> Nothing beyond reality. Within it,
> Everything. . . .[5]

---

[5] From "An Ordinary Evening in New Haven" in *Collected Poems,* copyright 1950 by Wallace Stevens. Reprinted by permission of Alfred A. Knopf, Inc.

(2) The Reconciling Image

To say that this world has come of age does not sufficiently indicate the new sense of insecurity which has accompanied its independence of tradition and custom. A series of radical shocks rising from the Renaissance subjected the heritage of the medieval world to devastating disillusionment. The structure of imaginative forms in which the world had organized itself collapsed. For the most part, the symbolism and institutions had been marked by a basic Christian significance, so when secular forces moved into the ascendancy and took priority over the traditional religious ideas, there was little left to hold the culture together. Negatively, the religious unity was lost; positively, the burgeoning powers of man's diverse activities, such as art, politics, science, and industry, all assumed autonomous pretensions. Religion no longer had a voice in anything except religion.

To be born into such a secularized world, to be educated in it, to make decisions of vocation and marriage, to grapple with its obvious contradictions and fascinating if not overwhelming diversity, is to bear the burden of its brokenness. What we have inherited is not a vision of reality, a persuasive and suggestive symbol of unity, but as Eliot has put it, a "heap of broken images." What once held the world together, imaginatively, has been battered and broken by the storms of history.

Few of us struggling with the immediate urgency of circumstance lift our eyes above the local scene to catch the significance of this disappearance of a framework of symbolic unity. We have easily assumed in a *laissez faire* manner that somewhere, somehow "all things do work together," without trying to make any effort to express such a faith, or we glibly and euphemistically praise the state of "pluralism" as beneficial and highly virtuous. To be sure, as an immediate observation, pluralism is the state of affairs in which we live, but religiously pluralism is not a statement of faith at all; it presumes merely a temporary form of polytheism. Ultimately faith affirms some kind of unity, or it is not faith.

When the writer of the Book of Revelation said that he "saw a new heaven and a new earth, for the first heaven and the first earth have passed away," he was indeed a fortunate man, for he had achieved a new vision of reality when the old one had proved obsolete. The metaphysics of Greek philosophy and religion no longer sustained the unity necessary for that enlarging world; in short, the old heaven had passed away. The speculative image suggested either by faith or by reason was no longer adequate. Similarly the old earth—the moral and political genius of Rome —simply could not support the complexity and scope of the "world" it had created and which had grown beyond it. Both in the realm of practical matters and in the projection of an ultimate reality from which society could derive its unity and authority, the ancient traditions were bankrupt.

Fortunately, the writer of Revelation was given a new image of reality. He beheld a new heaven and a new earth. Although the traditional writers of Greece and Rome no longer sufficed, there now was available a revelation of reality so much deeper and more comprehensive that, where they had failed, the new image formed a foundation for a much larger society, more complex in character and yet more capable of sustaining in unity those diversities and contradictions which brought Greece and Rome to an end. The image of Jesus Christ, crucified and resurrected, and the complex of symbols and rites that elaborated its meanings, became the fertile source of a new world, with a new metaphysic, a new ethos, a new institution. History was interpreted, nature was explored from a different point of view, man was re-evaluated, society was reordered.

It ought never to be forgotten that this large, complex symbol of reality was never in any complete sense an explanation. It contained an inner logic, that is, it reflected the kind of causal relationships men observed in their own lives at the human level. Its real satisfaction lay in the bold articulation by which the mystery was projected, and in that projection became something with which men could come to terms. It had structure; it was not altogether illogical; it made sense when taken in the light of much that men knew; but it was not science, not even primitive science, if that word is respected for its sheer objectivity.

THE FADING IMAGERY

The fading out of the great structure of Christian truth from the imagination of men has become one of the salient features of our time. That magnificent fabric, fashioned in concrete terms, which interpreted the ultimate nature of reality and elucidated the mystery and meaning of history, has slowly but surely vanished from the practical concerns of the modern man, and all too often from the preaching of the church. Beginning with the creation and the fall of man, ascending through the prophets and the psalmists, and reaching its climax in the revelation of Christ the Lord, with the last judgment as the final act, it supplied man with a vast and profoundly intimate formulary by which all the common events of the world and of his own life could be interpreted, judged, and held in meaningful unity. With the coming of the modern era, signalized by such names as Newton, Laplace, Darwin, Marx, man's gaze was turned away from that sacred panorama until it lost its focused sharpness and became a dim blur on the distant horizon of the primitive world. Sections of the structure came under the direct attack of evolution, natural law, and historical criticism. What was not demolished by argument slowly fell to pieces through the neglectful attrition of a world interested in other things. The ruins of that once majestic structure still stand just beyond the edge of our busy lives, but to most moderns they seem no longer habitable.

Milton was probably the last great writer or genius to utilize the Christian myth with appropriate strength and grandeur. But it is highly significant that his works, while much honored, are no longer widely read. Their structure of dramatic action, the pattern of motivation and moral reaction belonging to a Christian era, render them somewhat opaque to modern minds. His was the last glory of the setting sun before the coming of the long night. The breakup began and flared to a bitter anguish in Thomson's *City of Dreadful Night,* while the ruins of Tintern Abbey stand like a symbol of the lonely, listening soul of Wordsworth, who heard in solitude only the sad voice of humanity, bereft of those living metaphors and mighty signs out of which both faith and poetry are made.

In truth the old had not fallen away so much as it had been pushed out by the new. Sir Isaac Newton's myth of a universe so tightly contingent that no light of another world could shine through it had moved into the center of man's attention. Cause and effect now began to have a kind of numinous attraction for the human mind, and everything was laid under this new dispensation. Nothing was denied in sacrifice to the new god, and the old god was suddenly and literally out of a job. He no longer fitted into the framework of universal absolute contingency, self-operating and self-explanatory, which purported to represent the whole truth of reality. For a long time the Christian tradition would be respected, but within smaller and smaller perspectives. Its grand structure would remain, but its power would dwindle. Having fallen from theology to ethics, it would at last justify itself on practical grounds. Men would defend it, sometimes in extremely unfortunate ways, but like the gods of classic Greece, it was on the way out, to be treated with declining respect, made the butt of easy humor, and to have less and less to do with the morality of even those who maintained it in their sacred liturgies.

If we turn to ourselves, it is evident that we who live in the twentieth century cannot entirely hide from ourselves the painful realization that the old heaven and the old earth are passed away. How radical the change may be argued, but it is beyond cavil that the world is not the same today as it was in an easily remembered yesterday; nor, in truth, are we. The strain of vast social upheavals, the pressures of world-wide revolutions in thought and action, the anxieties and fears of catastrophic power, all lie heavy on us, whether we are young or old. To say good-by to an old heaven and earth is never easy, but to say it when we cannot as yet see the new is a trying test of our integrity and courage. For in the old we seemed to have security and permanence, and in its passing we are left with a frightening void. The world itself is no longer solid beneath our feet but shifts from day to day most undependably; and the heaven of our hopes and dreams has moved farther away from us than ever before and is confused by all kinds of uncertainty, so that we do not know what to count on near at hand or in the long run.

It is not strange that we look back nostalgically to an age where the vision of heaven and earth could be so definitively elaborated as in Dante's *Divine Comedy,* where all human experience from the deepest abyss to its noblest height could be accurately assessed in a vast and well-co-ordinated scheme of unity; or as in St. Thomas's *Summa,* where all human knowledge could be classified in a mighty plan, each item having its place and each place its validity in the over-all scheme. By comparison, we live in a sprawling, undisciplined jumble. For good or ill, the burgeoning power of modern man has shattered the patterns of that older unity and introduced us to a larger but more uncomfortable world. When in recent years James Joyce sought to recover the vision by which we might see things whole and in some kind of order—or as he himself said, to "rehabilitate the moral conscience of the race"—he was forced to fashion not so much a total image, with Dante's clarity and comprehensions, as a mosaic of countless odds and ends from the scrap heap of memory.

RADICAL IMPORT FOR SOCIETY

Not only is this a personal void; actually it represents one of the most radical problems of our contemporary world—socially, culturally, and politically. Lewis Mumford states the matter succinctly when he says that "the fatal course all civilizations have so far followed has been due, not to natural miscarriages, the disastrous effects of floods and diseases, but to accumulated perversions of the symbolic functions."[1] When the vision of reality, precisely the symbolic function, vanished from a people, that people literally fell apart. Society cannot sustain itself except by an image of unity from which it derives its coherence and sense of significance. This is corroborated by Werner Jaeger in his study of Greek culture and by Johan Huizinga in *The Waning of the Middle Ages*. In both eras the loss of vision preceded the disintegration of society.

Indeed, one of the places where chaos has manifested itself most plainly is in the artist. The traditional imagery of reality conceived of as signifying a certain integrity or consistency vanished about the turn of the century. There was no common world view, no consensus of what reality really was, no acceptable frame of refer-

[1] *Art and Technics,* Bampton Lectures No. 4 (New York: Columbia University Press, 1952), p. 51.

ence in a world of contradictory perspectives and purposes. Only one thing was true: the Christian form of unity and meaning which had ruled the imagination for centuries had relaxed its hold and no longer provided symbols provocative enough or of sufficient power and profundity to embrace the centrifugal disorganization of life and society.

The plastic arts particularly reflected this lack of a stable world and its basic cause, namely, the loss of an image of reality. The visual arts split into innumerable schools, each running off with a single aspect of beauty—one with light, another with Euclidean form, another with motion, and still another with color. The image of the world disappeared; form became problematic in itself; improvisation was highly valued; nonrepresentational art throve; the human figure tended to disappear entirely or to haunt the canvas in horrible caricature. In such a situation it is not strange that the artist, reflecting the nature of the world in which he did his work, seemed somewhat insane. There was simply no vision of reality available to support balance, to suggest meaning, and to nourish the kind of beauty which would recreate the world in terms of a higher harmony.

In religion the situation is not very different, although most people think it is. Religion has been confused by the viviparous forces which have splintered, not only the church into sects, but the religious image of reality into mutually exclusive relics of a once total, full-orbed Christian vision. Here, too, a basic world view has disappeared. We have specialized in form, color, law, spirit, or experience; liturgy, polity, or freedom. What embarrasses us is the atrophy of our symbolic imagination. For the most part it is assumed that imagination is to be associated only with the production of fiction. Reality on the other hand is best described by discursive or analytical reason. Images have been broken up to find out what truth may be in them from a literal point of view. Exactness, particularly in its objective or quantitative mode, is held to be of greater veridical worth than comprehension or adequacy. We simply no longer believe in the trustworthiness of images as instruments for the exploration or the expression of truth. Those we inherited from the past have fallen apart, and the resultant debris is assembled as interesting pieces we might use here and there as decorative touches of self-conscious nostalgia. But the image of wholeness is gone, chewed to shreds by the grinding pressures of prosaic exactitude.

PARALYSIS OF DISCOURSE

Indeed a kind of paralysis of discourse has overtaken us in the midst of this pluralistic specialization, in that every field of endeavor now has become a world in itself, with its own "field," its own method, and its own authority; moreover, in every aspect of man a special language has grown up, typifying the singular autonomy and freedom of such segments and managing now to produce a most bizarre sort of Babel, in which it becomes increasingly difficult for any educated man to talk with any other about the things closest to him, about which he knows the most. In ever broader terms the artist has a jargon the poet does not understand; the poet cannot make much of the words coined by science; and science in turn is in the dark about political or economic concepts. When it comes to religion, there is an assumption, of course, that this is a field in which everybody can read the Bible, identify his own experience, and pick up religious terms from the church easily enough to talk intelligently and be understood generally. But the truth is, the whole assumption is wrong. Modern man has been trained to think in the special terms of autonomous activities—in short, to think scientifically of nature, to think psychologically or socially of man, and to think entertainingly of art. As for religion, the usual approach is to think morally about it, in terms of its respectability value, or at best—if he identifies himself more closely—to think religiously about it.

In other words, religion is no more understandable today than modern art or advanced science. It has its own jargon, and it remains for the most part enclosed within the ecclesiastical field of operation. The connections between the Garden of Eden and our guilt-laden neuroses, or between the incarnation and science, or between the crucifixion and our peace, have been lost. The jargon means something, it sounds right at eleven o'clock on Sunday morning, but beyond that it seems out of place and will disturb a conversation as rudely as an unexpected obscenity. The images of art have been separated from the wholeness of life—we do not know what they mean religiously or politically. The same thing is true of the religious image of reality. Besides indicating whether we are Jew or Catholic or Protestant, what connection do such images have with the industrial juggernaut, with international conflict of power, with scientific research for bigger and better bombs?

The tenacity with which these enclaves become the sanctuary of rigid orthodoxy and arrogant dogmatics even in the realms of science and politics, is amazing. It is as if men, facing the breadth and fury of this total void, had to find a place in its terrifying speed, sudden changes, and erratic directions for security and stability, even if personal pressures have to be imposed to accomplish it. Where there is no reconciling image for the over-all confusion, man acts with understandable desperation to keep order in the smaller fields where he is able to maintain some degree of control.

A NEW SCHOLASTICISM

The attempt of the last three hundred years to substitute abstractions for an image of reality is obvious to anyone who glances back across these centuries. The secularity of which we have been speaking may be characterized as an historical act by which culture at the end of the medieval period had been exorcised of the plague of Christian symbols gone to seed, which had paralyzed all freedom and corrupted the vision of man, only to leave a vacuum into which rushed a mixed flood: on the one hand, a stream of ideas, opinions, abstractions, all rising from man's liberated reason; and not long after, a second wave of images derived from the industrial revolution. The latter soon glutted the world with a cheap imagery which took the place of the sacred imagery of the Middle Ages. At a higher level, we sought to satisfy ourselves with a prolific elaboration of speculative abstractions, which has become a vast and complicated web of ideas taken by many in our time as the true picture of reality. If the concrete forms of reality are ignored, however, then thinking tends to degenerate into a kind of artificial chess game, and ideas are endlessly spawned by interaction without reference to life, producing what Bradley once called a "ballet of bloodless concepts."

It is the image that keeps the connection between meaning and reality plain. The arts are the ways by which we continually pour the concrete, living world back into the symbols and shapes of meaning, or by such constructions elicit old meanings from new circumstances in the world. The lack of this "reality-intake" as Herbert Read calls it, impoverishes thought and leads to an obsessive fantasy with ideas abstracted and insulated from the embarrassing ambiguities of life.

When we turn to our religious life in this secular age, it is difficult, without incurring a large measure of misunderstanding, to declare that one of the strongest aspects of the secularization of religion is its dogmatic theology. The rationalistic influences of the seventeenth and eighteenth centuries tended to set the lines rigidly in terms of ideas. Out of the passion to understand, to have an idea of a thing, to verbalize it and talk about it at length, all this becomes a particular symptom in reducing religious realities to theological ideas and churches to gathered communities of persons who might have the same ideas about baptism or the soul or the Bible. There was simply no reverence left for a symbol or a rite which could span different ideas. Ideas were taken to be tantamount to reality.

When it came to theology itself in the strict sense, a new scholasticism crept into the enterprise. The revolutionary changes in the basic ways in which man thought of his world or of himself seemed to have had no effect whatever on theology. It pushed around the chessboard the same pieces or concepts without any fundamental questioning of their intrinsic meaning or function. The vocabulary of the world had changed drastically; the vocabulary of the theologians had not. Christological considerations, for instance, had completely ignored the entire dynamic system of the self discovered by psychoanalysis. The doctrine of God showed no altered perspectives, although it was clearly evident that earlier categories of the divine had risen out of innocent projections and unsophisticated notions of power and causality.

An even graver problem is that the theological enterprise has always reserved for itself not only a special province, which is legitimate and a matter of course with every science, but a special advantage which it denies all others. This is the privilege of revelation, which provides the theologian with the sacrosanct materials for analysis and all too often with the assumed authority of a special methodology in respect to religious truth unknown to man in other fields of inquiry. In the long history of Christianity, orthodoxy has managed one way or another to keep the world away from its privilege. For a long time Christendom suffered under the arrogance of an ecclesiastical idolatry in which the church assumed the sacrosanct role. When Protestantism revolted against this, it was not long before the Bible became the "paper pope." But even when biblical idolatry was broken, sophisticated scholars drew the theological circle around Christ in such a way that no earthly criteria could be applied. He became the *locus dei* shrouded in fire and cloud, and separated from history and the contingencies of this world. Even when this guard was relaxed, the same gambit was made in reference to revelation in distinction to religion, so favored of continental theologians. What is the fear that operates to guard God so zealously? Does He have any relationship to the remainder of history, or is He boxed in at these points in order to provide the theologian with a special privilege not accorded other truth-seekers, or even God-seekers? I am not denying revelation, but only the boxing it in, making it the special preserve of the theologian. Jacob Taubes has put the matter well. He says that

> the time has come perhaps when theology must learn to live without the support of canon and classical authorities. Without authority, however, theology can only teach by an indirect method. . . . Theology would have to remain incognito and not strive for the vainglory to present itself as exegesis of canonic scriptures and classical creeds.[2]

One discerns a long-postponed task, unwillingly faced, of dealing seriously with the world as God's creation. We have avoided this by centering our attention on the special "creation," on Christ, and the doctrine of redemption. The truth is that we have no doctrine of nature, and very little that could be taken seriously as a doctrine of creation in its contemporary reality. The world has been disdained theologically despite the Biblical precedents in the Old Testament which conceived of it as the handiwork of God. It would almost seem as if confidence in creation had passed from the hands of the church to the hands of science at the time of the Reformation.

That there are differences in the modes of truth no sane man would deny; but that religious truth is directly given and all other truth derived, I would deny. The speculative tautologies of contemporary theology are as fascinating as some of Rube Goldberg's famous contraptions for complicating simple action, and about as much concerned with real life.

THE DEGRADATION OF THE IMAGE

The resultant lack of satisfaction in the use of abstractions as adequate reflections of reality accounts in no small measure for

[2] "Theology and the Philosophic Critique of Religion," *Cross Currents,* Volume V, Number 4 (Fall, 1955), p. 329.

the glut of imagery. When real currency is scarce, counterfeit will proliferate without limit. Our culture, deprived of profound or truly sacred images, nevertheless swarms with images of all sorts.

Magazines are now full of pictures instead of words; television has taken the place of radio; the church world, public relations, and politics are agog with all manner of audio-visual aids and manipulated insinuations of popular images. Add to all these the vast spread of advertising with its highly charged images, suggestive, impelling, subtle or vulgar. Was there ever an age as incessantly machine-gunned and soaked in images as ours? All that once was poetry has now been vulgarized to assist in selling sausages, hair shampoo, and male deodorants. What once was magic held as a spell by wise men now is commercially available in a 99-cent bottle to make a bedraggled hag over into a stunning princess with stars in her eyes. If the poor serfs of the twelfth century had little to contemplate except the figures on the cathedral, or the crucifix at the crossroad shrine, now we can all sit for hours on end, morning, noon, and night, beguiled by beer cans, hand lotions, and aspirin tablets. We have images, plenty of them. They run from Cadillacs to filtered cigarettes, from pink telephones to swank hotels, murder, snakepits, and high-priced asininity. The only difficulty is that they are all cheap images, cheap in the sense of lacking richness of meaning. They have no depth, no height. They solve nothing, have no significance, are unable to pull life together. Instead they are a burden, a bore, a deceit.

What we are seeking is fundamentally *a reconciling image,* although the descriptive adjective is far from strong enough to describe the dynamic energy inherent in true symbols. Usually we consider a symbol or an image as a static object, a picture of a particular sort. Actually, however, even advertising in its crassest efforts deliberately counts on the dynamic intensity of certain images. Few of them have reconciling power. What we need is an image of such interest and depth that it can redeem life from superficiality and relate us again to the depths of our origin and the ground of our existence.

Herbert Read bluntly testifies:

> I can only presume to speak for a majority who regard this divided and tragic world we live in as devoid of any compelling image of reconciliation; therefore absurd. I think I still speak for a majority when I further assume that no compelling image of reconciliation is found in existing religions: or if it does exist there, is distorted by dogma and conventional behavior—by what Kierkegaard in his righteous zeal called an "impudent indecency."[3]

In the West, since the fall of Greece and Rome, the reconciling image has been the passion of Jesus Christ, symbolized by the crucifix and elaborated in the manifold events of his life, death, and resurrection. The long and extremely significant development of that image, its seemingly inexhaustible supply of new perspectives and fresh stimulation in the opening up of man's consciousness and the world derived from it, is the story of our Western history.

In the words of one of our profoundest psychologists, the "lesion from which man suffers is within the organism of man: That is to say a new humanism must look for its forms, not in the reorganization of man's social and economic activities, but in the structure of his psyche."[4]

THE LOSS OF TRAGIC DEPTH

Whatever it is that constitutes the potency of an image to draw together the uncomfortable and even frightening contradictions of this world, it must be said that the tragic nature of existence can-

[3] *The Form of Things Unknown* (New York: Horizon Press, 1960), p. 176.

[4] *Ibid.* Quoted from Trigant Burrow, "Emotions and Feelings," in Martin L. Reymert, ed., *Emotion and the Social Crisis: A Problem in Phylobiology* (New York: McGraw-Hill, 1950), p. 485.

not be evaded. This is what spoke so profoundly and perpetually to the ages from the Christian symbol of the crucifix. Here all the terror-ridden conflicts of human history met in One whose response transformed them, reconciled them in the sense that mankind, however perplexed by the rational questions involved, found an existential answer of such magnitude and strength that the stalemate on one level was broken and a break-through was afforded the human spirit.

It was when Western culture moved away from the tragic that the figure of Jesus Christ rapidly shifted to all sorts of thin substitutes—sentimental, intellectual, and pious—until in our time it no longer manifests any fundamental key either to the nature of reality or to the destiny of man. As our age became increasingly subject, first to optimistic romanticism and then to technological utopianism, the tragic nature of life was put behind men's backs and denied. The death of tragedy in our culture coincides with the rise of the doctrine of man's perfectibility and of social progress. When man turned his back upon the painful contingency of mortal existence, he removed from his attention the question for which Christ had been the satisfying image of reconciliation, implying a unity beyond the painful agony of opposites.

Under such conditions, the images which had reconciling power, which appealed to depths of experience not open to a rational solution, or contradicted the systems of rational theology, were dropped as superstitious or idolatrous. Images that consorted better with the growing optimism about man or the less tragic notions of existence, such as the Shepherd figure of Christ or the Lord of little children, became popular. Rationalism prepared the way for emotional compensation in pietism; the harsh iconoclasm of the Puritans was metamorphosed in the bland principles of liberalism that followed it. The job of reconciling this world's terrible and ineluctable contradictions, the tragic questions, simply was not touched.

Moreover, this loss of a powerfully reconciling image *left religion without a vocabulary*. To be sure, it had plenty of words.

Never in history had Christianity expressed itself so endlessly in perpetual sermonizing or ceaseless linguistics as during this period. It buried itself in words, and still does. It suffers from a disease of speech. Never have so many words been spoken with so little consequence. But words alone are poor counters in the exchange and communication of religious reality. They are at best shadows on the surface, of wings unseen and far above, at worst the whipped-up froth of hidden tumult. The image, by its symbolic nature, takes in event and meaning, sight and insight, history and destiny, reason and the unconscious, good and evil, suffering and resurrection, flesh and spirit, man and God, visible and invisible, past and future, time and eternity. It reconciles as discursive speech never can.

THE EFFECT OF SPEED

Another reason the images used in our time are lacking in depth and seldom penetrate to archetypal levels (or when they do, are immediately discarded as irrelevant) is simply the speed at which we live. The fury of haste with which we are impelled atomizes time and life in such a way as to isolate quite effectively every event and experience. Everything is made discrete, unconnected with a past or a future. It stands alone, with nothing under it. Going through experience as fast as we do, we have no time to probe beneath the surface, to hold an event long enough in our attention to break through to the sustaining mystery out of which it came, by which it is sustained, and into which it may pour its meaning and mystery. In a world as hell-bent as ours, hell is simply a void in which there are no images to support continuity or significance; life becomes a storm of shadows, dreaded in coming, haunted in going.

The extraordinary changeableness that affects every aspect of our life reinforces the sense of speed. The cinema with its exaggerated hop, skip, and jump technique by which nothing remains on the screen long enough for one to "see" it, to let one walk around in it and look about, is quite symptomatic and typical. Whereas in the days of the Roman Empire furniture styles changed every four hundred years, they now shift about every ten. The annual obsolescence of style in autos and TV's and clothes pushes the fleeting image faster. Today's earth-shaking headline on page 1 is on page 10 tomorrow and completely forgotten the day after. How can any poet, or artist, or prophet speak to people whose sight is caught in a horizontal blur of speed and never has a chance to probe beneath the surface of the thing seen, to the level where it may touch the substance in which seemingly separate and discrete things are bonded together in a union of mystery and meaning? In such a way of living there is no adequate time to develop the potential that merely registers as a "passing" experience and disappears into limbo without divulging its substance or significance. An image of reality is impossible under such conditions.

THE RECOVERY OF A RECONCILING IMAGE

The image for which we wait, or the image we must rehabilitate, cannot be one we consciously choose or rationally fabricate. It will not be elicited from the mysterious chaos of this tumultuous age by IBM computers or squadrons of slide rule operators. It will rise from the mist and the murk, the very nature of our obscurities, noiselessly and without warning, without let or hindrance, claiming our sight, riveting itself upon our imagination, fettering the profoundest necessity of our condition, as if it were the very gift of God directly to our need. Jung has said, "One is dependent on *symbols* which make the irrational union of opposites possible. They are produced spontaneously by the unconscious and are *amplified* by the conscious need."[5]

This is not to say it will not be resisted. Is there anything man has ever desired with his whole heart that he has not resisted with his brain? The very nature of our freedom leaves us inwardly di-

[5] C. G. Jung, *Answer to Job,* R. F. C. Hull, trans. (London: Routledge & Kegan Paul, 1954), pp. 175 f.

vided, tormented as often by an answered prayer as by one unanswered. We cry for some semblance of unity, we hunger for it and labor madly to produce it, yet we fear it too. In the split and shattered world we hide, now here and now there. We change our skins so to speak, appear in many guises, change our masks and costumes, dance to different tunes, leap from one setting to another. We like variety, playing out the manifold possibilities of our freedom with infinite—or almost infinite—zest. We are free enough to want no center, to shy from any fixed point, to break through any rule. We simply are not strong enough to will one thing, to bear with the one God, to reconcile everything with one purpose.

The new image is not likely to be a pleasant one any more than the crucifixion was pleasant. It must come carrying all the vulgarity and embarrassment of the human condition, displaying the nature of that evil from which we need to be redeemed, yet by which we declare ourselves to be human. Freedom must speak in its darkness as well as in its light. It will undoubtedly impress us as something in which no beauty is seen, as something despised, scorned, to be repudiated by anyone intent on keeping his reputation intact. It will come from the profoundest abyss, and with all the habiliments of human shame rise to the heights of divine blessing, when beauty and holiness alike are seen in a cleansing terror. It must somehow reconcile what we most dislike with what we most desire. God and the world must be in it, and nothing can be subtracted from either, or the result will be blasphemous or obscure, a pretty thing to hold before the eyes of the damned, but impotent to bless them.

Where will such an image be found? Perhaps in the church! Perhaps, because at times there has been in the church precisely this extraordinary breadth of reality which reaches boldly into the deepest hell and as supplicatingly into the highest heaven, and by its own pain holds the opposites in meaningful relationship. If it is to be found in the church, I cannot imagine a likelier place than in the act of worship. If this could be brought alive, if the dead, smothering blubber of respectability could be sloughed off it, if it could once again stand the naked soul before God, if the rushing torrents of man's sins and doubts could pour through his broken prayers, if a new honesty like a strong antiseptic could bathe away the suppurating sores of pious vanity and ecclesiastical foppery—in such worship of such men, human at every level, the image they have adored might come to life again and clutch their souls with eternal mercy.

On the other hand, it may not be possible to cut through the thousand layers of impervious self-satisfactions which the church has wittingly and unwittingly nurtured, down to the cosmic quick, where man is very man and God is very God. We may have to turn our back on the church in order to find what it once had and has lost. Indeed the world in all its lostness may at last save the church. For at present it is in the world, in the lost world, that art, the former and shaper of images, is at work. Seldom has there been such a frenzy of creation or such a chorus of testimonies articulated with devout, philosophical, and prophetic religious spirit. The artist is engaged in an engendering act, struggling in one medium or another to show forth that beauty by which unity is always named, and by which the peace that comes between God and His world is portrayed. The results may disappoint us, or even disgust us, but let us not miss the fact that what we do in the church seems as disappointing and sometimes as disgusting to the artist. His activity does not seem to fall into the traditional form of men at prayer, but it should be seen that he is actually the one who is engaged in the desperate struggle with the angels of mystery in the darkness of this world. He may seem quite savage, anything but ecclesiastically courteous; but the life-and-death struggle of making images deep and large enough to embrace the total scope of man's enlarged and unredeemed energies is unlikely to appear as a parlor game or a matter of "ruffles and snuff." Over and over again the artist may be blamed for fishing in these dark wells, but he cannot be satisfied with the superficial, however pretty. His destiny is to reconcile what is deepest in man with what is highest, what seems evil with what must be good. He, as few others, sees the damage done to man; indeed, such damage that some artists give up the human figure and revert to other structures to attain some sense of unity and beauty. Probably no artist has been more misjudged by Christians than Picasso, yet of all modern artists it is he who has stubbornly clung to the human figure as the center of meaning, revealing it crucified, plunged into hell, but equally glorified by a kind of Giotto-like holiness, unmistakably magnificent and simple.

It is no exaggeration to say that religion is lost without the arts. Whether the church can recover them soon enough to withstand the impending drift into a swamp of cultural pietism, a sort of secular *Schwärmerei,* remains to be seen. Without them the church has no language adequate for the enumeration or proclamation or communication of her essential realities and truth. Without art, faith is dumb.

We may continue to rely on abstractions, educating our members more and more in the skill of biblical research and theological elaboration, but abstractions, however rationally interesting and even exciting, will not save us or provide us with more than sophisticated ventures of the mind. With vast numbers of people rising from the confusion of the world and unsatisfied by its technological fabric and fury, we may try to win the day by more organization. And while it is inevitable that there will be more organization in such a culture as ours, it is dubious indeed whether man can be saved, his peculiar human quality in freedom and integrity of self conserved, by increasing the machinery of organization in the very place from which modern man may be seeking surcease from it. Once again we may depend on the historically dubious dictum that nothing succeeds like success, and manage to build the church into incredible dimensions of bigness and popularity. Yet I fear this may only make men tenfold more the victims of a demonic emptiness, children of the devil. None of these—abstractions, or organization, or success—will save us.

We need a reconciling image, large enough to hold all things, passionate enough to burn through all contradiction to an underlying peace, powerful enough to thrust beyond all petty separations to the magnitude of unity underneath them, compassionate enough to leave nothing in man outside its mercy or insight. It must be holy enough to bring God's blessing, hopeful enough to revive man's trust in life, and humble enough to force him to kneel. It must be rich enough in joy to celebrate in praise, honest enough to reach to the lowest level of earth, and sublime enough to climb toward the light that rests on the highest summits; touched with shame enough not to equivocate, and faithful enough to labor tirelessly at the endless shaping of the world to fit God's dream.

(3) The Point of Religious Atheism

When Dietrich Bonhoeffer in his *Letters from Prison* said that "our coming of age forces us to a true recognition of our situation vis-à-vis God, in that God is teaching us that we must live as men who can get along very well without him," he is drawing to a fine focus the absence of God from the secular world.[1] The miracles and the epiphanies have ended; the prophets and the saints are superseded; the church has ceased to trouble itself with mysteries and has skilfully achieved worldly success. The mumbo jumbo and the magic have been eradicated from rite and symbol, and in their place sophistication and respectability rule quite decorously. God has ceased to disturb the ecclesiastical routine by so much as a shadow of the divine presence or the embarrassment of a too flagrant interruption of the social proprieties. As Martin Buber

[1] Dietrich Bonhoeffer, *Letters and Papers from Prison*, Reginald H. Fuller, trans. (London: S.C.M., 1954), p. 163.

put it in the arresting title of his book, there is an *Eclipse of God*.

One must say, I think, that the secular age, having lost its sense of unity, yet striving for nothing else quite so much, both in its theoretical science and in its practical frenzy of organization, is withal a godless age. Popularly conceived, secularism is a synonym of godlessness.

Hegel once remarked that the nineteenth century lay under the curse of a speculative Good Friday. Many others, among them Nietzsche and Dostoevski, have corroborated this godforsakenness. Most men in the nineteenth century were still tipping their hats and inflating their high-sounding rhetoric in God's behalf, somewhat condescendingly it is true, but with a degree of sincerity as far as such courtesies go. The Victorians and Junkers in their highly decorative life were not touched by what seemed Nietzsche's lunatic announcement of God's death. The magnitude of the crisis, its emotional impact and denouement, were much more profoundly sensed by Nietzsche himself, when he described the situation.

> Where is God? I will tell you. We have killed Him, you and I. We are all His murderers! But how did we do it? How did we drink the ocean? Who gave us the sponge to wash off the entire horizon? What did we do when we separated this earth from its sun? Whither is it travelling now? Whither are we travelling? Away from all suns? Is there still a height and a depth? Are we not wandering towards everlasting annihilation? Do we not perceive the indications of this immense void? Is it not colder? Is not the night becoming darker and darker? Must we not light our lanterns at noon?[2]

Later, in *Joyful Wisdom,* he writes:

> The most important of more recent events—that "God is dead," that the belief in the Christian God has become unworthy of belief —already begins to cast its first shadow over Europe. . . . To the

[2] Quoted from "The Gay Science" in Walter Kaufmann, ed., *The Portable Nietzsche* (New York: The Viking Press, 1954), p. 95.

few at least whose eye, whose *suspecting* glance, is strong enough and subtle enough for this drama, some sun seems to have set, some old profound confidence seems to have changed into doubt: our old world must seem to them daily more darksome, distrustful, strange, and "old." In the main, however, one may say that the event itself is far too great, too remote, too much beyond people's power of apprehension for one to suppose that so much as the report of it could have *reached* them; not to speak of many who already knew what had *really* taken place, and what must all collapse now that this belief had been undermined—because so much was built upon it, so much rested on it, and had become one with it: for example, our entire European morality. This lengthy, vast, and uninterrupted process of crumbling, destruction, ruin and overthrow which is now imminent: who has realized it sufficiently today to have to stand up as the teacher and herald of such a tremendous logic of terror, as the prophet of a period of gloom and eclipse, the like of which has probably never taken place on earth before?[3]

A CHANGE IN ATHEISM

Although we have not yet taken such men seriously, we know now there has been a change of climate in the world. A generation ago, Joseph Wood Krutch, in the preface to *The Modern Temper,* said of our age that "one of its most distinguishing features is just its inability to achieve either religious belief on the one hand, or exultant atheism, on the other." Today that is not true. A line of major thinkers have accomplished precisely an exultant atheism, an atheism which in fact possesses all the exultant aspects of religious belief itself.

Susan Anima Taubes more recently characterized this fact by saying:

Atheism, which used to be a charge leveled against skeptics, unbelievers, or simply the indifferent, has come to mean a *religious* experience of the death of God. The godlessness of the world in all

[3] Friedrich Nietzsche, *Joyful Wisdom,* Thomas Common, trans. (New York: The Macmillan Company, 1924), p. 275.

its strata and categories becomes, paradoxically and by a dialectic of negation, the signature of God and yields a mystical atheism, a theology of divine absence and nonbeing, of divine impotence, divine non-intervention, and divine indifference. Religious atheism is distinct from secular atheism from the start, in that it invests the natural world, from which divine presence and providence have been totally excluded, with theological significance. He who, seeking God, does not find him in the world, he who suffers the utter silence and nothingness of God, still lives in a religious universe: a universe whose essential meaning is God, though that meaning be torn in contradiction and the most agonizing paradoxes. He lives in a universe that is absurd, but whose absurdity is significant, and its significance is God. God, however negatively conceived, explains the world, explains the nothingness of God in the world.[4]

She continues to point out the revolutionary causes for such a change, ranging

from the critical investigation of sacred Christian history to the final shattering of faith in divine providence in the moral catastrophe of the twentieth century. They encompass the scientific technological transformation of a hierarchically created universe into a blind mechanical process; the empirical investigation of the religions of the world leading to the relativization of Christian dogma and institutions; the progressive undermining of faith, first by Marxian theory, that exposed religion as political ideology, and then by psychological and psychoanalytical theory, that reduced "religious experience" to behavioristic and subjective categories. The scientific conception of the universe and the critical inquiry into the nature of man and society have relegated religious "symbols" to the level of useful or useless, dangerous or therapeutic, fictions.[5]

In a world where everything happened by law, where cause and effect were utterly ubiquitous, where there was not the slightest chance of anything happening other than that which had been determined by its antecedents, however complicated they might

[4] "The Absent God," *Journal of Religion*, XXXV, 1 (1955), p. 6.
[5] *Ibid.*, pp. 6 f.

have been, there was literally no room left for God's action. This can be most clearly seen in Simone Weil's writings, where absolutely nothing escapes the rule of determinism and where this becomes God. This she calls "gravity." Furthermore, in such a world, where telescopes and microscopes had swept us all into a very sophisticated space-time continuum, there was no place left for God. He became unthinkable, unimaginable, unplaceable. Perhaps this is what we mean by an apocalyptic or eschatological age. The conditions of thought and faith are radically changed. We simply do not know how to think of God. He no longer acts; we do not find Him responsible for anything; we do not fear Him. He is away. Yet we remain capable of religious fervor and expression. We fill the void with aimless posturings and gestures which we would direct if only we knew where the right direction lay. Indeed, our very fervor is an extreme expression of our desolation. The fervor becomes contagious, and a popular religion hides the loss of God with frantic but superficial piety.

One can see the beginnings of the process in Marxism. It is a commonplace among scholars that this most virulent and dynamic atheism of our time had within it, strangely enough, the characteristic aspects of the very religion it purported to deny. By a philosophical inversion of Hegelian idealism in which Christianity was to be rationalized, Marx managed to inculcate the ancient categories of faith in the modern materialistic dynamics of class conflict. The chosen people became the proletariat, the messianic era was ushered in by their victory, and the kingdom of God was achieved by materialistic means. Here was a religion without God. Of course this had been prefigured by others, particularly Feuerbach, who had suggested that God was merely the projection of those powers which had always inhered in humanity itself. The infinite and eternal categories of divine life really referred to the inexhaustible resources of the human race.

There is another cause for God's absence. One might put the matter directly by saying that it is not so much a change in God but a change in man that produces the "death" of the divine. Humanity has moved into a different level of life where God's actions are no longer visible. They are actually hidden by our way of looking at things. The very position we take, the methods we use, the perspective of seeing and understanding are such that God is no longer visible or intelligible. What we have done is to substitute completely the attitudes of science for the total range of man's responsiveness to reality. This reduction of sensibility to one stratum of existence, our growing inability to think except cognitively, analytically, causally, is indeed a very critical change in the nature of man's capacity. Other portions of our psychic life, which flourished before the rise of science, have been excluded from serious consideration as possible means to the truth. No wonder E. M. Forster, the English novelist, has said that "modern man is developing in ways which science cannot comprehend and theology dare not contemplate." This is what Berdyaev seems to be saying when he asks if the creature who will inherit the modern world deserves the name of man.

The cult of objectivity (so vividly analyzed by Nietzsche), the emptying of inwardness, the depersonalization of man, the externalization of his life in a technological age, his degradation by the technics of the modern era, all point in the same direction. God may be there, but *man is not.*

Several other historical forces have assisted in generating this climate in which religion grows more intense and God less meaningful or real, among them the fact that Protestantism itself has been extremely iconoclastic, attacking all forms, symbols, and analogies as if they were superstitious idols. This radical "protest against Form" can be traced through its successive surges of rational abstraction and liberal sentimentality. In pietism God disappeared in formless emotion; in idealism He disappeared in faceless concepts; in liberalism He disappeared in abstract principles; in pragmatism He disappeared in the popular demand for practical success.

RELIGIOUS RESPONSIBILITY FOR ATHEISM

Now the point of religious atheism in our time will not be visible as long as we stare blindly at the shocking idea of rejecting God. Something much more complicated has happened. To a large degree atheism has come to be, if not the theoretical position of many, the practical condition of multitudes who accept God in a verbal sense, but do not know what to do with Him in any existential reality. Atheism at its best (and there are different kinds of atheism), when it is not merely an emotional superstition, is really a criticism of the predominant opinions about God. "Every religion," as Jean Lacroix has said, "can degenerate into superstition, and every representation of God which is not purified by critical atheism can become idolatrous."[6] In short, atheism usually appears in the world as the void left by inadequate representations of God. When religion fails to give an adequate image of ultimate reality in the symbol God, then men, by reason of their honesty in the light of truth, must become atheistic and often in their atheism will affirm realities that are religious. God was not rejected in a satanic mood with unbridled gestures and profane heroics. Nietzsche's notion that we have been responsible for God's death does not mean that we deliberately planned to reject Him or even knew that we had done it. Indeed, there is a suggestion that those who are most shocked by the idea of God's death were the most implicated in it.

What was it that deafened man to God's subtle presence? What blinded him to the signs of His activity? What changed man's stance so that he could not see God from where he was standing? How did he rearrange his life so as to topple God—to put Him off, so to speak, so that there was little chance of meeting Him?

I suppose, after we get over the first refusal to admit it, that we shall have to confess finally that we killed God. By "we" I mean most explicitly We Christians. We domesticated God, stripped

[6] Jean Lacroix, "The Value and Meaning of Atheism Today," in *Cross Currents*, Volume X, Number 3 (Summer, 1955), p. 205.

Him of awe and majesty, trapped Him in nets of ideas, meticulously knotted in a thousand logical crisscrosses; cornered Him ecclesiastically, taught Him our rules, dressed Him in our vanity, and trained Him to acknowledge our tricks and bow to our ceremonial expectations. After some time, it was difficult to see any difference between God and what we believed, what we did, what we said, or what we were. God and *our* Church, God and *our* morals, God and *our* belief, God and *our* class, God and *our* feelings, God and *our* scruples, God and *our* vanities—all were one. So much so that it seemed plain after a while that we were deceiving ourselves. God of the *mysterium tremendum,* the God of holiness and of wrath, had vanished—God was not really there. We had effectively done away with Him; somewhere, we did not know quite where, we, the worshipers of God, the Christians, had buried Him. And the tragedy of it is we still act as if God were present. If we are honest men, we can hear what Kierkegaard called "twaddle" in the Holy of Holies—prayers that have no more sense of God's mystery than if they were grocery lists for the errand boy at the local *Stop and Shop;* sermons of such impeccable inanity that their profanity sounds like the sacred language of heaven itself.

The iconoclasts cleared out the rubbish of superstition, but they prepared the way for empty abstractions to take the place of a real God. The pietists wanted nothing more than to know God inwardly, to feel Him spiritually, sensationally; yet they ended by seeing Him no longer in the creation He had made, but only in their self-manipulated emotions. The liberals wanted to understand God intelligently, rationally, but before they were through they had reduced Him to a harmless and impotent set of principles. God was killed by His friends.

To be sure, there were other factors, but none of them as effective as the attrition of superficial devotion. Where men thought they possessed Him, could live with Him comfortably and complacently, and managed by one means or another to use Him as a buffer between themselves and reality, there God died. Science assisted the iconoclasts, going further than the iconoclasts had ever intended, cleansing the universe of all but mechanistic process; romanticism encouraged the feelings to express themselves in all directions without limit, as if feelings did not need to be rooted in reality to be authentic; education pushed liberalism beyond itself, creating a whole world of abstract ideas accumulated by a strange lust of research, valued as data and stored ponderously in the silent Babels of bursting libraries.

There is no doubt that at the present juncture we are feeling the shock of the collapse of traditional idolatries. We have carried them far beyond the time of their due end. Out of sheer inertia they extended their rule long after they had lost their power, and in sentimental devotion we kept the appearance of their reality propped up long after the substance of it had evaporated. The forces that changed the size and shape of the universe did not have to attack the deities our vanity had made in comfortable proportion to our own size; in the blinding light and unimaginable dimensions of the new world, they were simply lost.

The inability to move quickly to a bold spiritual renovation of our notions bequeathed an evil conflict to men. Such a world left us with no respect for such piddling gods; or, if we kept such gods, they had to be protected by devious means from the reality of such a world. So the gods retreated from one frontier of mystery to another until the rout became comic and somewhat meaningless. More and more of the world was taken over by science, and religion was left less and less space for God until it was no exaggeration to refer to Him as unemployed. Julian Huxley averred that He was like the smile of the Cheshire cat, which would soon be erased from the universe.

A novel by Alan Weichert called *Jeromin's Children* tells of the disappearance of God as it affects four generations of the Jeromin family. It begins with the atheistic great-grandfather who stands upon the street corners and fulminates most dramatically against The God he so heartily despises and denies. By the fourth generation, however, the fervor of atheism cools and in Jumbo, the great-grandson, it completely vanishes. Jumbo is comfortably, thoroughly, completely adjusted to a natural world, a world without intimations. He is completely "free of all ill feeling or complaint against fate." He is not disturbed by any fundamental mystery. Everything is accepted at face value. Existence is taken to be a complex of facts, but nothing more than facts. There is no depth, no height, no beyond or within. He no longer raises the religious question. In fact, he is unaware of it. Jumbo is as credulously at home in the world as a saint might be in the will of God. The two are alike in that neither has any rebellion in him. They are both adjusted perfectly, though it is to different realities. This is a bland kind of atheism, not uncommon in our churches.

THREE RELIGIOUS ATHEISTS

In *The Castle* Franz Kafka, in a much more profound and significant way, also tells of God's absence. While this book is extremely controversial as to the intent of the author, I think one can safely deduce the fact that "K" is searching for some empirical evidence of a transcendent factor in experience. He does not feel himself altogether a part of the world in which he must live, yet he cannot find the structure of meaning that would make sense out of his life. He has abilities, but they never seem to be totally employed in the work he happens to find available. He keeps busy in many ways, gets involved in love and hate, persistently and cunningly lies in wait to meet the messengers from the castle, but in all these things he never attains the clear-cut approbation of authority for which he hungers. In brief, he is a man trained and conditioned by scientific modes of thought to be a surveyor and to put things in their places with great precision, but his hunger exceeds this and for the very life of him he cannot perceive through this method the ultimate satisfactions he desires. This, in brief, is the dilemma of modern man, a structure within man himself demanding faith for its fulfillment, limited by a structure of interpretation called science, which he has lifted out of the nonhuman world and now seeks to impose on the peculiarly conflicting realm of freedom where God and the world meet in himself.

While Kafka deals with the empirical search for some transcendent meaning in the web of human experience and fails to find it—always and everywhere, however, making evident the hunger for it—one of the most provocative philosophical minds of Germany has been describing the phenomenological structure of human being. He has described what it means to be human. I refer, of course, to Martin Heidegger, who has striven to establish an ontology in his now famous and very crabbed *Being and Time.* And, of course, it is particularly significant, for it is Heidegger's philosophy that stands in back of Bultmann's theology. Man is described by Heidegger as the only creature related to itself. This primordial act of transcendence is the foundation, both practical and theoretical, of reality. It allows for freedom, decision, the fall of man; for authentic and unauthentic modes of existence. Thus man is related to his own death, and his whole life determined by this proleptic force. His conscience becomes the method of his choice of possibility, the appropriation of himself. But in this realm of dread occasioned by freedom, decision, and death, Heidegger completely encloses man within himself. As Buber shows in his study of recent anthropology, the dimensions of reality beginning with Hegel dwindle as they pass through the thought of Kierkegaard down to Heidegger, where there is nothing outside self. The world and God have vanished to reduce man's dimension to the intrapsychic distance of relationship with his own death, the sign of authenticity. In a sense, this has all the marks of a religious interpretation of man—the categories of freedom, authentic and unauthentic existence, the fall, dread, decision, conscience, choice of death, concern—and yet, no God.

Since *Being and Time,* however, Heidegger has continued in such a way as to suggest that the very lack of God is itself a revelation and a promise. In his interpretation of the poet Hölderlin, he describes the present as a time of need, because it rests under a double negation, the no-more of the gods that have fled and the not-yet of the god that is coming.

Each torpid turn of the world has such disinherited children
To whom no longer what's been and not yet what's coming, belongs.[7]

It is the acceptance of this interim, the between darkness in which we remember revelation and hope for revelation but must wait without power to create revelation, that constitutes our particular destiny. As Blackham puts it, Heidegger

> seems to think of the total renunciation of the resolved personal existence described in [*Being and Time*], steadfastly nullifying all realizations without refusing them, as in its perfected purposelessness a form of purification which draws close to Being and, as it were, makes way for Being, by making oneself over to Being; one is serene and listens to the silent voice of Being and bears witness in the world to Being. . . . This meets the need of the age, the age which is no-more and the not-yet of the gods, the age when the meaning of the question of Being has been so completely concealed by knowledge and lost sight of in the perspectives of an active civilization that it does not make sense any more.[8]

This severe *ascesis* of Heidegger is matched by Simone Weil in a most dynamic way. She criticizes the "Christian doctrines of the immortality of the soul, resurrection, divine providence, and eschatological hope as forms of consolation that are obstacles to faith." To endure the absence of God is to be purified; it is "fidelity to the void," "loving in the emptiness." "God," she says, "is absent from the world, except through the existence of those in this world in whom His love lives." Thus to affirm and deny at the same time God's existence is a "case of contradictories which are true. God exists, He does not. Where is the problem? I am quite sure there

---

[7] Rainer Maria Rilke, *Divine Elegies*, J. B. Leishman and Stephen Spender, trans. (New York: W. W. Norton & Co., 1939), p. 63.

[8] Harold J. Blackham, *Six Existentialist Thinkers* (New York: Harper & Brothers, 1959), p. 105.

is a God in the sense that I am quite sure nothing real can be anything like what I am able to conceive when I pronounce this word." In short, for Simone Weil the dark night of God's absence is itself the soul's contact with God! To endure the void . . . is our contact with God. Her own words are: "The Absence of God is the mode of divine presence which corresponds to evil—absence which is felt."[9]

Let us pull together some of the glimpses we have had of this remarkable phenomenon. For Kafka, man is haunted by a terrible and unremitting need of God, which none of the experiences native to this world satisfy and without which he suffers degradation. For Heidegger, the nature of being human is self-enclosed on every side, and without hope save in death itself. To accept nothingness is the purification that may prepare the way to Being, the rebirth of God. For Weil, the world is as ambiguous as for Kafka, a vale of suffering for which God is undeniably responsible. It is as contingent as in Heidegger. But here Weil daringly closes her fist on the hardest affirmation of all—the acceptance of the void not as a way to God; it is God. Grace is to endure it as void, not as a way to something better. Salvation is in the cross, not in the resurrection; in affliction, not in liberation.

FOUR THEMES IN ATHEISM

It would be impossible to follow all the trails suggested by even this cursory examination of a religious atheism. Let us point briefly to four. The first theme that runs through most of the religious atheism since Nietzsche's announcement of God's death is the burden of this world. The great grinding machinery of nature, the iron necessity of law, the ubiquitous web of determinism, the everlasting contingency of everything—this is seen and known and felt as never before. And with it is the tragic, the meaningless, the absurd—Ivan Karamazov's "tears of little children"—none of

[9] Simone Weil, *Gravity and Grace* (New York: G. P. Putnam's Sons, 1952), p. 72.

it to be ignored, plastered over, perfumed with abstract sentimentality. The full brunt of the world as a world has been faced—and must be faced if faith is to be more than an escape.

Secondly, in religious atheism there is an attempt to reckon more seriously with God as the creator of this world. The seriousness is indicated in the "yes and no" of Heidegger and Simone Weil, in the tenacity and open-eyed precision of Kafka's nightmare vision, in the honest gratuitousness of things in Sartre. No matter what the price, no matter how deep the mystery goes, God cannot be conceived apart from the nature of the world and the realities we perceive in it.

Thirdly, the embarrassment of conceiving God is patent in all the instances I have mentioned. God to be God must not be the world. God's freedom must be postulated in some way without removing Him from the world. (Barth's attempt to maintain the freedom of God in the Wholly Other must paradoxically end in the Humanity of God.) Berdyaev's insistence on God's arbitrariness is certainly near the juncture of significance, but also nearer mysticism than meaning. Karl Heim's "nonobjective" space is another fruitful suggestion. Buber's reality of the "betweenness" is still another. And Marcel seeks the same freedom in what he calls the "exigence of transcendence."

One sees again in Heidegger, Jaspers, and Weil the *via negativa* of Plotinus. Moreover, this is the circle where the structure of miracle must be fought out again if God's freedom is to give meaning to the Christian categories Simone Weil so brusquely discards.

In the fourth place there is a powerful element of nonidolatrous faith in much of this thinking. The intellectual *ascesis* is extremely severe, presenting higher pressures than ever before upon the simple images of the Christian faith. Faith in this structure is to be measured by its penetrating depth of doubt. Few can hold these powerful contradictions with integrity. They are much like the Abrahamic sacrifice of Isaac, and not always conceived as Kierkegaard conceived them in the double movement of Isaac's return.

AFFIRMATIVE FACTORS

But now we must turn from this thick negativity and its varying implications of religious intentionality to ask if it is possible to assert affirmatively the nature of faith in God for our particular time.

In the first place, there is a positive act involved in the honest repudiation of idolatrous clichés, however ecclesiastically blest they may be. To get rid of this false mask of deity, fashioned more or less like man himself at his most pompous moment, whitewashed or pacified to deny the responsibility for this kind of world, or rendered inane by smoothing out all the inexplicable mystery and tragedy of existence—to get rid of this is positive in the sense that we get nearer to dealing with the true transcendence. As Alfred North Whitehead declared so clearly in his *Adventures of Ideas,* "Progress of religion is defined by the denunciation of gods. The keynote of idolatry is contentment with the prevalent gods."[10]

With the discarding of old and very respectable idolatries, the world itself was seen in a new light. Scientific objectivity, disciplined in terms of accuracy and clarity, cleansed nature of a thousand superstitious delusions and eventuated in a world more susceptible of order and man's control than ever before in history. Miracles, ghosts, demons, epidemics, black magic—all the ragtag bundle of fuzzy fear-filled projections and fantasies were eliminated, leaving a rather "clean" world. By contrast, of course, it seemed an impersonal world, a world of objective things, natural events, normal routine, plain circumstance. Otherworldliness dropped away, the fear of hell diminished; royalty disappeared, as well as pomp and circumstance; rhetoric descended to plain prose; machines took over the role of power, and man was absorbed by vast collectivities; the world became pragmatic and less and less romantic.

Yet this is still the world God made—this plain, disenchanted, *C*-major world, without signs and wonders of fiery portents or

[10] New York: The Macmillan Company, 1933, p. 12.

ghostly messengers of hell. Under our stupid fears and our paranoid distrust we have found a world more amenable to understanding at certain levels and cleaner for thought and reflection. But the ineluctable mystery of its existence is still there, swept bare of all its superstitious haberdashery. A secular world is no less mysterious than the old world punctuated with fitful jabs and starts of divine epiphanies, and its mystery may be as holy. Moreover, it will be seen as the holiness of a world which God created entire. We come close to some of the mysteries, to Genesis itself, to Dostoevsky, when we reach the point where we affirm, not the separate acts that disclose God's presence but the whole creation, whose mystery celebrates His goodness in every stick and stone, in every star and soul.

Our temptation at this juncture is to move much too quickly! If the old idolatries which were formulated out of our sinful vanity, making God omnipotent because that is the way we would like to be, were we God, or omniscient because we would want to know everything if we were God, are outgrown, then let us make a new image of God! How strange we are! Delivered out of the hand of one idol, we rush to form another. It is good to remind ourselves of Tillich's admonition: "We can discern God at the very moment when all known assertions about God have lost their power."[11] Or again, we must remember Pascal: "Every religion that does not affirm that God is hidden is not true."[12]

This is the juncture where we must learn one of the most difficult disciplines of the spirit. How to remain at the point of need, to stand persistently, stubbornly at the haunted center where the hunger is most intense; not to be tempted or distracted or lured away by facile hopes and wild surmises! This is the hardest thing in the kingdom—how to be poor, to know one is poor, to patiently bear the burden of poverty, not to reach for the spun coin, the

[11] Paul Tillich, *The Protestant Era* (Chicago: Chicago University Press, 1948), p. 203.
[12] *Pensées,* W. F. Foster, trans. (New York: Random House, 1941), Frag. 584, p. 191.

glitter of sudden wealth, the proffer of alms. When God is not here, then it is better not to play as if He were. If He cannot be found, then let us wait until He returns; let us not play with ghosts to deceive ourselves and others. If He is silent, then let us be silent; He will not remain so forever.

Waiting is painful, but it is not deadly. It is not stagnation or passivity or idleness; it is of all spiritual activity a most affirmative intensity. Let it grow—in silence. Do not speak God's name; let the reality absorb the name, overwhelm it, drench it, and drown it until glory and grace stream over it on all sides.

But can we do more than wait, though the waiting be done in the most affirmative activity of the spirit we can manage? What are the acts of a soul who has been painfully delivered of old or common idols? Can faith, while waiting, en route through the wilderness, find reason to lift its voice in praise? Is there not a biblical precedent in the notion of the *deus absconditus,* which intimates that there is something paradoxical in what we have called the absence of God? Perhaps this absence is not so much God's death as man's attempt to capture God in a place, to identify Him by custom and tradition. It may be that for the first time we have a chance to "believe" in God, in the God revealed by this event, this time, rather than merely to imitate the response of earlier men to earlier occasions.

As Paul Ramsey points out in his preface to Vahanian's *The Death of God:*

> Contemporary men should banish nostalgia and freely engage in the cultural enterprises of this present age premised as it is on the death of God. It is not impossible that fundamentally the freedom to go with this culture in its independence may be the only way to go with a God who is at all a living God. or the "living" God means the 'freedom" of God. The radical freedom of God in His own transcendent life apart from man means that man has room to breathe.[13]

[13] Paul Ramsey, Preface to Gabriel Vahanian, *The Death of God* (New York: G. Braziller, 1961), p. 29.

We begin to touch God when we move beyond the limits of any event or person to that essential mystery which sustains them and at the same time transcends them. We need in truth a new vision of nonspatial transcendence. Wherever one moves through the narrow gate with perception and insight for the eternal; wherever one breaks common bread, but with it all the tender and eternal holiness of love and death; wherever one draws his breath, not merely to fill his lungs with air but to let the universe circulate in the limitless systole and diastole of the part and the whole; wherever one picks up his cross and with it all the pain and indignity of the world, and by a mystery no man can avoid, calls all men to share in the cleansing power of His compassion—wherever such things happen, however men may use God's name or discard it, there He is believed. God is that to which a man appeals when he gives himself to any single event or passing circumstance or humble passer-by so totally, so fully, so wisely that the moment is brought to fullness, its destiny completed, its glory revealed. God is always hidden, always weak, always "least in importance."

To have faith in God is to act any time, anywhere, as if the gift of one's whole self were justified though the circumstances deny it and the conditions are unfavorable. It is, in short, to believe in becoming, in the limitless possibilities of becoming, in the kind of becoming that transfigures men and transforms the world. It is to believe when there is no proof, even when there is little promise, perhaps when there is little or nothing to be gained.

What is the holiness of nature but its possibility, the very mystery of its becoming? What is the *deus absconditus* but the God who is hidden in the plain routine of causal structure, waiting for fulfillment in the transcendent spirit of man? Fundamentally there is no religious work—that is, there is no other activity for faith—but that of dealing with the secular world so that the implicit may be made explicit, so that its holiness may be revealed and God may be disclosed, not anciently but modernly, in a new place, under circumstances as yet unlabeled.

The church may well keep alive the memory of those events in which God was revealed, not as heirlooms no longer operable, to be stored in a museum, but as reminders of our present duties. The vanity of a church in love with itself comports scandalously with the fact that God so loved the world—this secular world—that He gave His only begotten Son, that whosoever believeth in him might be saved.

THE COST OF FAITH

To be sure, faith in God, like any high emprise of the soul, is costly. One must be purged of comfortable idolatries and sentimental inanity; one must be humbled and made willing to submit to this contingent world, to serve its smallest need and its most commonplace event, to stoop in meekness to human need, if the reality of God is to be manifest. Even more, one must expect to suffer. This is a hard saying, but it is imbedded in the gospel deeply, and it is inextricably woven into the very fabric of Christian history in the image of the cross.

But there are many kinds of suffering, and an effort must be made, however clumsily, to distinguish the kind that expresses faith in God. The world is filled with the tangled knots of evil and pain, of evil hated and pain endured, of pain cursed and of evil born of pain. The perplexity and mystery of suffering are endless. But there is a suffering which comes to the soul when it perceives the glory that might come to pass were this event or that person brought to fullness. This is the highest love, to see beyond the limit what will only come into being if long and patient labor is endured. The artist knows this; his soul is contorted with the pain of hunger to shape this stone to speak that beauty. The saint knows this; his life is thrust down and he cannot help but kiss the leprous sores to bring mercy to the ironbound captive heart. The poet knows this; the tender membranes of sight are touched with all this world's anguish in order to hear one silver drop of dew in a flower bell or the wrenched flutter of a leaf that floats to earth from its hold upon the sky. If you believe in the kingdom where everything might become a miracle, where all men might become new creatures in God, where the world itself might be restored in paradise, and you are willing to suffer that it might be so, then you believe in God.

I do not know why grace has been so dissociated from suffering in theology. To be sure, it is full of joy, a supernal joy of amazing buoyancy and light; and yet I think that grace and suffering must be seen together. It is by grace that the world of nature is redeemed, and there is no redemption except by the cross. No poem is written, no picture painted, no music made, no sinner forgiven, no child born, no man loved, no truth known, no stone shaped, no peace attained, except grace took a risk, bore a burden, absorbed the evil, and suffered the pain. This is believing in God, too.

Indeed, there are two things about God perennially unavoidable. He is most certain in the deepest mystery; though He grants no information, He does give His presence. And secondly, we never see Him directly; He is always mediated by the very things that seem to deny Him. What these things mean is that the incarnation and the crucifixion and the resurrection are not separate events; they are phases of believing in God. We share in the world, ineluctably; we bear its sins, its shame, and its agony, for good or for ill; and if by the power of the spirit we know what we are doing, the resurrection is our daily hope and glory.

A story taken from an essay by Erich Heller on Oswald Spengler and the predicament of the historical imagination illustrates the matter well.

The late Munich comedian, Karl Vallentin—one of the greatest of the rare race of metaphysical clowns—once enacted the following scenes: the curtain goes up and reveals darkness; and in this darkness is a solitary circle of light thrown by a street-lamp. Vallentin, with his long-drawn and deeply worried face, walks round and round this circle of light, desperately looking for something. "What have you lost?" a policeman asks who has entered the scene.

"The key to my house." Upon which the policeman joins him in his search; they find nothing; and after a while he inquires: "Are you sure you lost it here?" "No," says Vallentin, and pointing to a dark corner of the stage: "Over there." "Then why on earth are you looking for it here?" "There is no light over there," says Vallentin.[14]

Perhaps—and I only venture a guess—the key we are looking for is likely to be in a place unilluminated by academic street lamps.

Or one might turn to W. H. Auden, where he says:

> For the new locus is never
> Hidden inside the old one
> Where Reason could rout it out,
> Nor guarded by dragons in distant
> Mountains where Imagination
> Could explore it; the place of birth
> Is too obvious and near to notice,
> Some dull dogpatch a stone's throw
> Outside the walls, reserved
> For the eyes of faith to find.[15]

At the last, we must say that when the world becomes a wilderness, despite its chrome-plated conveniences, bereft of meaning and of God, then the only way back to God is through man, not through the stars or through the past, but through man, the living center, the crux between God and the world, where all things are brought to nothing or raised to glory.

---

[14] Erich Heller, *The Disinherited Mind* (Philadelphia: Dufour and Saifer, 1952), p. 154.

[15] From *The Age of Anxiety: A Baroque Eclogue* by W. H. Auden, copyright 1946, 1947 by W. H. Auden. Reprinted by permission of Random House, Inc.

(4) Loss of the Human Center

Yeats' now famous line—"Things fall apart; the centre cannot hold"—announced another feature of our secular age. It is as if there were no longer a true magnetic north, but momentarily, without warning, the compass swings wildly hither and yon to the weird impulses of a disorganized energy. The popularity of pluralism reveals the fact that a center may be found anywhere, and with a little ingenuity and enthusiasm a pattern organized around it, at least temporarily. Centers may be said to be everywhere, in anything, regardless of strength or stability, ready for making fad or fiction, fun or fury. The frenzy that fastens upon this world and organizes it with such desperation is precisely a sign that we have lost the real center. We try to insinuate a center where there is none, and thus the patterns we make fall apart as soon as we take our frantic hands from them. And then, of course, their collapse creates anxiety and fear, and the drive is on again to reorganize the pieces around a new arbitrarily chosen point.

In *The Disinherited Mind* Erich Heller describes this condition accurately.

> . . . in the sphere of art the symbolic substance, dismissed from its disciplined commitments to 'reality,' dissolves into incoherence, ready to attach itself to any fragment of experience, invading it with irresistible power, so that a pair of boots, or a chair in the painter's attic, or a single tree on a slope which the poet passes, or an obscure inscription in a Venetian church, may suddenly become the precariously unstable centre of an otherwise unfocused universe.[1]

Such incoherence deprives the individual of any stable direction or permanent structure of loyalties; it loosens up the whole fabric of society, a loosening that can be mellifluously described as mobility or restlessness, but actually makes a dangerous kind of instability, easily exploited by political messiahs and nationalist fanaticism. In such a condition, the state is forced to exert more and more pressure to hold society together. The whole situation is permeated at every level, large or small, by flux that defies stabilization. Therefore, true community declines while collectivities in the way of huge cities or megapolitan areas increase. In the individual this leads to a kind of moral vertigo, in which purposes shift overnight and are so short-lived that they amount to a bewildering purposelessness. Persons become rootless, lured and driven by vagrant words and moods, unable to attain permanent relationships even in the family.

THE SHIFT OF THE CENTER

What is becoming increasingly evident, however, is not only that we do not possess a stable center around which life or culture can be organized, but that a radical shift of locus has occurred from the human center to any number of external activities. A kind

---

[1] Erich Heller, *The Disinherited Mind* (Philadelphia: Dufour and Saifer, 1952), p. 165.

of Copernican revolution has been taking place by which man has been slowly edged out of the center of the universe and quite subtly derogated to a secondary or ancillary position. To say, as Gabriel Marcel does in his description of dehumanization, that man has become a "function" is a clear indication of what is involved. He is no longer considered originative, or determinative, or redemptive. He simply exists at the edge of things, participating in them as all other things participate, by accepting them and adjusting to them.

Nowhere does this process become so obvious as in the visual arts. By World War I the human figure had become so difficult to handle that large sectors of aesthetic sensibility reflected the loss of the human center. Mondrian resorted to Euclidean and geometrical perfections; Kandinsky to extemporizations in color apart from form; the abstractionists to all sorts of concerns with nonhuman constructions. Oskar Kokoschka, shocked by what he called the incurable disease that had attacked modern man, said in 1945:

> Modern portrait painting has become a difficult task—since the artist who tries to make people see the human being, invisible in the present-day man, is apt to make a fool of himself. Since society is at present a mathematical and bureaucratically-concerned mass organization, we cannot hear the last bell toll, although the Apocalyptic Riders already shake heaven and earth. . . . Since Humanism is dead, man is soulless, he no longer cares whether he lives or dies. The march of industrial civilization will be marked with utter ruin and destruction, like the path of the hordes which once invaded Europe. There will be no portrait left of modern man because he has lost face and is turning back towards the Jungle.[2]

Where the artist could not completely exile the human figure, he subjected it to extraordinary distortions and violence. No one spoke more brilliantly or boldly than Picasso, affirming with all

[2] Quoted by J. P. Hodin in *The Dilemma of Being Modern* (New York: Noonday Press, n.d.), p. 69.

the vehemence of his genius that the human center was undergoing revolutionary attack. The resulting forms, to be sure, have shocked and, to a large degree, have not enlightened the blind. These prophetic probes have met the usual rewards of stones and epithets. In our own country, De Kooning's work is illustrative. The human figure is literally, visually, in a state of mangled shock!

Perhaps an easier, yet no less tragic, view is presented in Oliveira's canvases. Here a figure moves through a world of wisps and fog, an undefined, seemingly empty, swirling world where nothing is solid, firm, or fastened. And the figure itself, the man, has no face. He, too, is undefined, a cipher, a nobody, lost, lingering, alone, without home or hope of rest. Look at Picasso's "Les Saltimbanques" or Giacometti's "Pointing Man," or Kafka's K in *The Castle,* or Camus' Meursault in *The Stranger.* They are all infected—infected by a disease which puts man back into the shadows, off on the sidelines away from the real game, and brings him precisely to "nought." It is a world where man feels he amounts to exactly nothing. This is the course of nihilism, not in theoretical terms, but in man's concrete and historical situation. The vision is too unmistakable in the arts, in drama, and in the novel to be gainsaid if we were inclined; but our hearts tell us even more poignantly that the abyss has opened up, not between the stars, but in ourselves.

FORCES DISLOCATING MAN

How did the locus of significance shift from the human center to the world? Alienation, to use Hegel's term, is an historical event, not merely an individualistic neurosis. Powers and principalities have pushed man out of the center; he is dispossessed, an alien, a stranger, an "isolatoe"; the world has overwhelmed him, pushed him under, and he has now turned out to be a nobody in spite of his stupendous achievements. Indeed, the irony of it is that his very accomplishments have become the centers of life, and he, their creator, is left to serve them like a slave.

It is not difficult to see this process in the development of science. It reduces man to an observer and increasingly disciplines him to remain in the background as far as possible, lest he affect in the slightest degree the marker readings of natural phenomena. It is evident that this habit of withdrawal spreads and deepens while truth looms ever larger in terms that leave man out altogether. Technically and theoretically this is not true, as any simple reading of the theory of relativity shows, but practically and culturally the consequences are too obvious to be denied. "Objectivity" is the highest goal of science; man reads himself out of the center of such truth.

Moreover, it is not difficult to see that something of the same sort happens in the industrial system. As Karl Jaspers puts it:

> The new world which has arisen as an apparatus for the supply of the necessaries of life compels everything and every one to serve it. It annihilates whatever it has no place for. Man seems to be undergoing absorption into that which is nothing more than a means to an end, into that which is devoid of purpose or significance. But therein he can find no satisfaction. It does not provide him with the things which give him value and dignity. That which, amid the needs and stresses of the past, had persisted as an unquestioned background of his being, is now in course of disappearance. While he is expanding his life, he would seem to be sacrificing the being in which he realises his own selfhood.[3]

There are three things in the industrial revolution which dislocated man from the center—the machine to which he becomes a handle, organization by which he is placed in a system which the machine dictates, and things produced in such number and by such means as to deprecate his importance.

The way in which the machine has taken priority over man is so near us we may not see it very clearly. The fact that the machine is superbly ingenious, extraordinarily powerful, and well-nigh in-

[3] *Man in the Modern Age,* Eden and Cedar Paul, trans. (New York: Anchor Books, 1957), p. 83.

exhaustible, entertaining us, lifting our burdens, and increasing our powers, may hide the truth that we have become its tools, spending most of our time taking care of it and finding out that for the most part it sets the speed, determines our wants, and shapes our satisfactions. With speed alone it has changed the tempo of human life, accelerated it to the perilous point of being a compulsive obsession. Everything must be *Faster! Faster!* till man finds himself acting like a machine, disregarding the human aspects of fatigue or reflection. He tends to lose his abilities for a deeper penetration of events and persons for the sake of rapid superficial contacts and ground coverage.

If the machine takes over the center and calls the dance for man, so the ethos of machine efficiency and patterns introduces a new mode of human relationships. Man as such is pushed out of the method of relating himself to work or worship, in order to speed up relationships or to increase their number. Speed extrapolated from the machine into the world of community produces organization. Organization is the mechanical method of relating people to one another in the fastest possible way. It is the total order that counts, not the individual person, and the total order looks more and more like the machine: well balanced, completely powered, smoothly operating, with no excess motion and no sportive items. The men who share the motions in such organizations tend to become "interchangeable" parts.

Organization is a quick substitute for redemption. When two people are related—and it takes time, reflection, imagination for that to happen—then both are changed, whether they like it or not. In organization, people merely make contacts, and the result is that no one is changed. The redemptive vitality in human relationship is dropped out; there is not time for it. It is easier for a church to organize three thousand people than to redeem one of them.

Just as with speed and organization, the pressure of mass production tends to bury men under a welter of *things*. They lose sight of the richness of the human element and rage madly in a world overflowing with playthings. They lose their inner wealth and substitute the dubious clutter of machine-made junk. They are smothered by a Woolworth world. We are like Mickey Mouse in Disney's clever portrayal of *The Sorcerer's Apprentice*. We have said the proper words to produce the flood, but now we do not know how to stop it. The Machine pours out its profusion, and we are exhausted trying to keep up with it, stimulating our desires to want more, inventing ways to make things break down sooner so we can buy new ones, running pell-mell, dizzy and bored and disgusted and trying to seem happy, beside the assembly lines and wrapping counters where we go through the ritual of obedient slaves to a god we inwardly curse.

Yet it is not only science and industry that have pushed man from the center. Strangely enough, education does the same thing. The twin powers of science and industry culminate in a kind of abstraction, before which man retreats. Education, despite its intention and high devotion to the development of ability, suffers also the influence of abstraction, often becoming anything but the light of truth in which a man finds his place in the mysteries of this world. Instead he is beguiled by a kind of quantitative scholarship in which he accumulates hordes of data, processes them with due regard for organization, and becomes himself a veritable museum of ideas, a warehouse of facts—but for all that, having managed to avoid any profound maturation of his mind and spirit.

A fascinating illustration of this is contained in Gustav Flaubert's *Bouvard and Pécuchet*. In reviewing the novel, Lionel Trilling draws attention to the author's description of it as "a kind of encyclopedia made into a farce." It is a novel describing the ideological nature of modern life. What adds to the fund of social intelligence is the

> awareness of the part that is played in our modern life by ideas—not merely by assumptions, which of course have always played their part in every society, but by ideas as they are formulated and

developed in books. . . . If we try to say how the world has changed from, say, two hundred years ago, we must see that it is in the respect that the conscious mind has been brought to bear upon almost every aspect of life; that ideas, good, bad, indifferent, are of the essence of our existence.[4]

Ideas are life and death to Bouvard and Pécuchet. They are not imbeciles; indeed they are ridden with ideas, but there is no depth of thought in them. They have a lust for ideas, all kinds of ideas, any kind, from anywhere, for any purpose. They finally end up as copyists, the "Travailler sans Raisonner," the virtue of work without philosophizing.

Such secularized individuals tend to think of themselves as subject to external factors, worked upon by forces outside, possessing no intrinsic or determinative power—merely the effect or consequence of prior circumstance, not the origin of anything new or the unique ground of specific events.

THE BIBLICAL CENTER

It is precisely the sense of an inevitable and quite inescapable center, rooted deeply in man, that characterizes the biblical notion of the *imago dei,* or the Christian conception of the Christ. To lose this is the "lapse into anonymity." In its starkest sense, it means to lose one's soul. The substantive difference between man and animal disappears. The sudden coalescence of multitudes into a formless society which has no interior reserve eventuates in a pathological state of collectivity, a shapeless, unstructured mass controlled by external political means and ruled by fears and fantasy. This is the *Massenmensch,* whom Nietzsche so greatly dreaded.

There are few factors as markedly significant in the intellectual life of Western culture as the widespread phenomenon of existen-

[4] Lionel Trilling, *The Opposing Self* (New York: Viking Press, 1955), pp. 177, 179.

tialism when it is seen in the light of man's dislocation from the center of reality. Basically a revolt against the excessive abstraction of philosophy, particularly in its idealistic development in Hegel, existentialism has turned to a serious consideration of the human being who does the philosophizing. Kierkegaard's violent attack upon Hegel because he had completely liquidated the "individual" opened up a new inquiry (not without historic precedents) into the central problem of the relation of truth to the conditions of being human. Whatever we may think of existentialism as philosophical inquiry, it nevertheless represents the recovery of the human center.

The religious affirmation of the human center of reality is Jesus Christ. Strangely enough, as obvious as this ought to be, historically it is subject to many corruptions and heresies in which its truth is lost. Man veers away from such a burden of responsibility, freedom, and destiny. It is easier to push the figure of Jesus Christ into the supernatural realm, to substitute it for the awesome and transcendent God, to reduce it to a divine *Einmaligkeit*. It was, I believe, the twelve or fifteen centuries of persistent meditation on the nature of Christ that produced the extraordinary transformation of human consciousness in the Renaissance. It can be seen nowhere more plainly than in Michelangelo and Rembrandt.

The subtle complexity of Christology has made it extremely difficult to make adequate or precise affirmations of the meaning inherent in the Christ symbol. Thus the affirmation of the Christ as the theological affirmation of the human center of reality appears to be a reduction of the historic assertions in which the divine is included. Yet one cannot affirm the total meaning of the human without the divine. The perennial heresy which threatens us is the affirmation of the divine without reference to the human. One cannot make any sense out of affirmations which supposedly are pure of all anthropomorphic references, however subtle they may be. Whatever the divine means, it means in reference to human experience of some sort.

The very character of Jesus Christ as revelation means that he discloses the function of all men in their relation to God and the world. Anything less than this makes him into a historical surd of no earthly use whatever to any of us. He is the revelation in that he makes transparently plain the relationship of God and the world. In him the world is being reconciled to God. He—the human center, where transcendence and time meet—is the atonement. In him, man's vocation as human being is revealed for all time.

THE FADING IMAGE

Now the theological symptom that parallels the lapse into anonymity or the loss of the human center is the fading image of Christ. To be sure, his name is still praised, his life is elaborated, his words are preached, but withal the potency has so far left his figure that artists generally find it easier to indicate the mystery of man's life and destiny through clowns, or miners, or nobodies. His figure has been rubbed flat by custom and routine; he neither shocks nor surprises. He has been thoroughly domesticated. His mystery has evaporated, his power vanished, his thrust broken. We have finally absorbed him, made him our own, and dare to reshape his countenance to fit our depraved and vulgar tastes. Look at Sallman's pathetic arrow collar ad of him, or Dali's vaudevillian caricature of the crucifixion! The image, once filled with the terror of beauty, the very power to bring any man to his knees in judgment, has been smoothed and fondled to a safe blur. He, too, has suffered the same fate as the rest of us, pushed out of the center. He belongs to a world long gone, where all things were weighed at the human center; not in machines, or abstractions, or meter readings, but in the tender, pain-stricken heart of man himself.

It was Dostoevsky's unequivocal declaration that "the West was losing Christ; that is why it is disintegrating." Indeed it might well be that the figure of Christ has been competing for man's loyalties with science, the abstract god; with the machine, the mechanic god; and with research data, the intellectual god! Perhaps all of them fascinate us by their exactness, precision, power, and infinitude as over against Christ's weakness, his suffering and death, the common embarrassments of man. The question, however, could well be asked whether any world can long sustain the precarious being of man in his freedom and faith except by an image or symbol in kind. Are we not preparing our nemesis by whoring after these metal beasts, these mathematical gods so omniscient and so omnipotent?

Some of the responsibility for the increasing impotence of the Christ image belongs to the church itself. We have abstracted it into an absolute. By all manner of speculative logic, we have eradicated every earthborn reality from his being. In the very language in which we have asserted his humanity, we have managed to deny the ambiguity of his existence, the weakness and shame which were intrinsic to this human nature. He crowded God out so far that he took priority, as if God could not be known at all except by him. His uniqueness rivaled God's and was pressed to the limit, so that one was left wondering what such once-for-allness could say to the rest of history. Christ made into a demigod is no help at all to secular man, and for much of the last century theological language has put Christ far out of reach for anyone who stands within the structures of thought and life in the twentieth century.

Ecclesiastically the same thing has happened, not in theological terms, because the church of our time has been singularly lacking in theological imagination, but in the general tenor of devotion. A kind of unitarianism has grown up in which God has become extremely vague and shadowy, withdrawing into the background, more or less like a tired old man, to make way for the opposite thrust of pietism. In the liturgical churches as much as in the free church, the figure of Christ has been sentimentalized; the divine implications, the transcendent power, the apocalyptic judgment all eliminated. He became all Jesus, very soft and malleable, something less than a demigod but a bit like a talisman that could be hugged close to one's little self without fear of disclosing one's own reality.

There is another aspect to the fading image of Christ and that is the peculiar fact that, during the late nineteenth and early twentieth centuries, the "quest of the historical Jesus" which at its outset promised so much, finally ended ironically in the assertions of scholars like Bultmann and Tillich that actually the historical Jesus is of little moment or significance. It was the Christ of faith that counted. So little could be identified with certainty in the original documents, one was forced to build upon the interpreted notions which were found woven inextricably in the earliest stories. It is difficult to see how "Christ" could be kept without some evidence of the historical embarrassments that characterized the Christian insight that God is deeply involved in the very structure of human life.

If we turn then to ask what it is that constitutes the human center, in theological language it is Jesus Christ. It is true that if in our culture the human center goes, then Christ must wane; and if Christ is either transported beyond the human condition or absorbed by it, then the human center disappears. The two are vitally related.

CHRIST THE RECONCILING IMAGE

But one must go further. Jesus Christ is the reconciling image by which all things are united. In biblical language, he came to reconcile the world to God. This act of reconciliation, pulling together the refractory and contradictory elements of this mortal world into the fullness and meaning of God's purpose, was effected by means of freedom, imagination, and suffering. In so far as he makes this work and function plain, it becomes the work and function of man as such. We, at the human center, have the same function, no more, no less. We are to reconcile this world, in all its terrible and tragic conflicts, with the purposes of God in holiness and righteousness. And we cannot do it except by the exercise of our freedom seriously and responsibly considered, and by our imagination, transforming the possibilities of the world into unity, and by suffering the cost at every level of our being to bring all things into meaning.

By freedom, I mean that man is of all creatures the most permeable by the infinite aspects of the universe in which he lives, and the most permeative in his power to shape and change. The world is real, but it achieves reality only in man. In the human center, and there alone, it is rendered invisible and then transfigured in freedom to mean in man what it can never mean by itself. The world operates by law; man by freedom. In man the world becomes free, and in the world man's freedom becomes meaningful. The world has no destiny outside man, and man has no freedom outside the world. The religious declaration of the human center or of Christ is the affirmation that the function of religion is to fulfill the possibilities of the world. Religion is not to be concerned with itself; that is spiritual incest. The world is the whole concern of the church. Christ is not found by ascending to some exalted sphere of pure spirit or ecclesiastical glory, but by facing human life in the web of mortal necessities.

In back of the miracle tradition of the Gospels, I believe we may presuppose certain events in which the world was reconciled to God, or, if you will, in which the implicit nature of the world was explicitly fulfilled by a union of man's spirit and the world's possibility. What those events looked like to disinterested observers was what we would call natural events, no different from any other in the long process of cause and effect. But what they were in the life of the person whose freedom became the ground of their fulfillment, thirtyfold or sixtyfold or a hundredfold, was another matter. So crowded with meaning, the event could only be described by distorting the physical dimensions of it, as when we use a metaphor in poetry.

Thus it is that bread and wine became sacrament, water became baptism, and the cross became salvation. A sacrament is another view of the same thing seen in miracle. Ultimately, sacrament is a ritualistic attempt to repeat the conditions of the miracle. But neither miracles nor sacraments are by this token unnatural or magical events opposed to life. They are the completion, making explicit what is inherent in the nature of life itself. They are neither added, nor intruded, nor imposed. They belong to the fullest measure of reality. Without them, man's freedom would be empty and the world's nature would be incomplete.

Imagination is in a sense the active exercise of freedom. It is in the expectation that the whole creation groaneth and travaileth in pain till the sons of God be revealed. It is the perceptive readiness to meet the longing of the world by such insight and humility that each new event is treated as an opportunity to fulfill God's will. It looks within the event, unfolds it patiently, stays with it lovingly, and to the fullest extent elicits its total reality and significance. This is the work of the artist and poet, the true philosopher and the saint. It is also the work of the true Christian. Only when man gives himself completely can the world be fulfilled in its ultimate significance; reality is revealed in the wedding of man and the world. And Christ is precisely that reality made explicit and unmistakable.

It was Bonhoeffer again who declared that union of God and the world in Christ in ways that bring light to the Christological question.

> There are not two realities, but only one reality, and that is the reality of God which has become manifest in Christ in the reality of the world. . . . The whole reality of the world is already drawn in into Christ and bound together in Him. . . . The world is not divided between Christ and the devil, but, whether it recognizes it or not, it is solely and entirely the world of Christ.[5]

.   .   .   .

[5] Dietrich Bonhoeffer, *Ethics*, Eberhard Bethge, ed., Neville H. Smith, trans. (New York: The Macmillan Company, 1959), pp. 63, 64, 70.

Man is challenged to participate in the sufferings of God at the hands of a godless world. He must therefore plunge himself into the life of a godless world, without attempting to gloss over its ungodliness with a veneer of religion or trying to transfigure it. We must live a "worldly" life and so participate in the suffering of God. . . . To be a Christian does not mean to be religious in a particular way, to cultivate some particular form of asceticism (as a sinner, a penitent or a saint), but to be a man. It is not some religious act which makes a Christian what he is, but participation in the suffering of God in the life of the world.[6]

Nowhere is this made plainer than in the crucifixion-resurrection. This is the symbol of the cross which implies the necessity of suffering, the refractory reality of human evil, and at the same time the promise of meaning, deeper than death, the glory undimmed by shame.

But the difficulty of restoring the figure of Christ as the symbol of the human center is going to tax our imagination to the utmost. The tide of cultural interest is running against it on many fronts. Religion itself has been so extremely rationalized that it is not likely to recover the archetypal vision to rehabilitate the figure of the Crucified. Indeed the church is likely to develop still further in the direction of an educational agency with a new enthusiasm for courses in Bible and theology far exceeding anything we know. And on top of everything else, the kind of culture we have developed and probably will continue to augment is in the direction of comfort, convenience, and congeniality at any price. How can the suffering servant commend himself to such an overstuffed philosophy as now controls our motives, mores, and manners?

---

[6] Dietrich Bonhoeffer, *Letters and Papers from Prison*, Reginald H. Fuller, trans. (London: S.C.M., 1954), p. 166.

(5) The Inner Resonance of Life

Thus far we have come to see that secularity has a double meaning; the world on one side seems saner, and yet on the other it has lost meaning. It has more power, but scarcely more control. It has gained knowledge, but to a large degree lost wisdom. Its sophistication at every level has increased, but not its satisfaction. It travels with great speed through space, in action, and in change, but it lacks direction and penetration. It is proudly skeptical and yet it has nourished the most outrageous superstitions. It has few or no ideals and yet it is incurably optimistic. In technics it is incredibly ingenious, in politics unbelievably paranoid, and in religion hopelessly infantile.

Now that we have reached the state of secularity in all its advantages and negativities, and have come to reckon with the dislocation of the human center, what shall we say of the function of religion in such a culture? What can be said of faith in a world where faith itself is suspect, either as a medieval hangover or a neurotic fantasy? Can faith operate sensibly, meaningfully, appropriately, in such a secular world? A recent art magazine, in its initial editorial, declares that "the characteristic of the modern world is its inability to sustain belief." Certainly the traditional structures of faith—the church, worship, prayer, the figure of Christ—all have lost their numinous power. They neither frighten nor fascinate us any longer.

It is a strange thing how the instruments of faith in one age become worthless for another. Words and acts which held such power that life was redeemed from fear and futility, almost overnight seem empty, the life gone out of them, nothing left for sustenance or support. It was at such a time that the Reformation found and fashioned new words and deeds appropriate to man's anguished need and capable of real assistance to his spirit. They were instruments of considerable daring, of no little risk, and required of men a certain heroic stature of soul. That multitudes have retreated from them, being lured by the lush influences of a comfort-loving time, is obvious.

If we are to find our way back to faith, it is obvious we must rid ourselves of much obscurity and many false clichés. We do not want a pat on the back, a shot in the arm, a bit of eyewash to make the world look better. We want no humbug of any kind, certainly not of a religious sort. To smooth life out, to take out the terror, to remove the shame, to resolve the confusion until everything is easily understood, because what we cannot understand is hidden or repressed—this is not faith. Faith does not seek safety, logically or ecclesiastically. It does not take refuge behind infallible propositions or facile proofs or special revelations.

Job faced a world in all its naked contradictions. He simply could not find God under the circumstances and he was sickened by the silly comfort men tried to make out of fake answers. If all we want is a divine protector of our privileges and prejudices, a sure-fire refuge against every consequence of our own stupidity and malice, a convenient *deus ex machina* to pull us out of every dire emergency—then we are not acting in faith at all, but in superstition.

This is a powerful age, powerful in its vast knowledge and ingenious techniques, in engineering and manufacturing, transporting and utilization of natural energy. Yet in spite of all this there are some things we lack, much to our pain and impoverishment. One of them is the ability to believe. We investigate, analyze, observe, gather evidence, draw conclusions, prove, and—all in all—are extremely capable in the field of criticism. But to believe is something else. There we are like strangers in a foreign country, like fish out of water. How tempting to make our religion over into scientific, or rationalistic, or social terms, postponing the fundamental issue of believing! For believing is the very ground of the Christian experience. For many, their faith seems to be determined by how much they can prove to themselves is true; to others it must be said that they are able to believe so much more than what can be proved. In each of us this painful struggle of belief and doubt goes on, believing one day only to doubt the next. How do we extend the power of believing? We do believe, but all of us would like to know how to "help our unbelief," which not only limits but sometimes tortures us and deprives us of the peace our believing ought to give.

Our world is both hungry and overfilled; hungry for faith and sick of it. To many, faith still smells of superstition, of dark medievalism, of a surrender not altogether commendable in a mature mind. Multitudes have found it easy to substitute many things in its place, so that we have more opinions and less conviction, more sophistication and less culture, more contacts and fewer relationships, more philanthropy and less religion, more faith in work and less work in faith. And all the while, in the very midst of such an attempt at self-satisfaction, there is a gnawing of inner discontent, a sense of profound impoverishment in the midst of a world proud of its plenitude, its achievements, and its violently optimistic activities. Prejudiced against faith, yet hungering for it!

Let us turn from this great pandemonium of a world hung together with machinery, a world bereft of both devils and angels and grown so full of dread because the mighty gadgets of power may blot us out. Let us turn also from the great sanctified clutter of holy things which are supposed to be believed, a clutter of big and little bones, of white racks and empty skulls, tangled and interlaced, a veritable maze of the vestigial remains of prophet and saint and patriarch. Let us turn as most men turn today, tired and weary of too many things required all at once, too many cards up our sleeves, too many hidden hooks in the bait, too many assumptions and too many evasions of honesty; let us turn and see if there is any simplicity we can get our hands on to clarify the complexity of faith, the act of believing.

THE RESONANCE OF THE WORLD

Let us begin by describing faith as resonance, that dimension of reality in every event and thing which provides the possibility of reverberating to the sound of other events and other things. There is a resonance between man and the world; they are not only related, they are dynamically moved by each other; they hear each other. There is a resonance between the spirit and the flesh; each causes reverberations in the other, and thus spirit sanctifies the flesh, while flesh makes the spirit real. There is a resonance between God and the world; they fulfill each other, God speaking through the world, and the world finding its answer in God. At every level of life, in all events and circumstances, resonance is the reality of a ubiquitous relationship by which the world may be reconciled to God.

Indeed, "resonance" is one of the underlying structures of experience, one of the dependable references in the life of the spirit, in one of the greatest religious poems of our time, namely, T. S. Eliot's *Four Quartets*. The poem opens on the note of time's mys-

tery, the mystery of the past, present, and future and their strange
relationships, and then moves to that brilliant passage:

> Garlic and sapphires in the mud
> Clot the bedded axle-tree.
> The trilling wire in the blood
> Sings below inveterate scars
> And reconciles forgotten wars.
> The dance along the artery
> The circulation of the lymph
> Are figured in the drift of stars
> Ascend to summer in the tree
> We move above the moving tree
> In light upon the figured leaf
> And hear upon the sodden floor
> Below, the boarhound and the boar
> Pursue their pattern as before
> But reconciled among the stars.[1]

Or later:

> . . . as a Chinese jar still
> Moves perpetually in its stillness.[2]

Here is that structure of interrelatedness which characterizes
religious thought, an openness by which all things are held in an
infinite transcendence, sustained by the services of an everlasting
mercy. Nothing is self-sufficient, although the lower in the ranks
of being one descends, the less open forms become. The Chinese
jar may be forever still, its form definitive and final, yet even in
its deceptive stillness it vibrates, and a thousand years hence and
half a world away it will move to fill with pulsing beauty the waiting soul of man. It has the power to reverberate where there is a
space, a hunger, fit for resonance. This is the mark of meaning,

---

[1] From "Burnt Norton" in *Four Quartets* by T. S. Eliot, copyright 1943,
by T. S. Eliot, reprinted by permission of Harcourt, Brace and World, Inc.
[2] *Ibid.*, p. 7.

the beginning and the end of faith. The hunger of man is not left to starve; the world fits his hunger as food satisfies his need.

LOSS OF RESONANCE FOR CHRIST

The truth is we have little resonance for Jesus Christ. It is very difficult to believe in him, to reverberate to his reality. He was a man in whom God was reconciling the world to himself, and that required suffering, inner agony, extraordinary humility. What we want for the most part, and find it easier to believe in, is some kind of surrogate perfection, someone who never wavered, never doubted, never sinned. We want an absolute, no mixed or halfway measures; we want invulnerability, if not in ourselves, at least in our Captain, in our Lord, in our Boss. We want proof undeniable, a guarantee divinely given, a fixed assurance. How hard it all is, and how lacking in resonance! If it were that way, faith would be superfluous.

Indeed, it is a bit sad when we put ourselves next to Jesus, as an ear is put next to the mouth to hear what is said.

He was careless about himself, we are careful. He was courageous, we are cautious. He trusted the untrustworthy, we trust those who have good collateral. He forgave the unforgivable, we forgive those who do not really hurt us. He was righteous and laughed at respectability, we are respectable and smile at righteousness. He was meek, we are ambitious. He saved others, we save ourselves as much as we can. He had no place to lay his head, and did not worry about it, while we fret because we do not have the last convenience manufactured by clever science. He did what he believed to be right regardless of consequences, while we determine what is right by how it will affect us. He feared God, but not the world. We fear public opinion more than we fear the judgment of God. He risked everything for God, we make religion a refuge from every risk. He took up the cross, we neither take it up nor lay it down, but merely let it stand. He was a scandal, a scandal to the Jews proud of their tradition, a scandal to the scribes proud of the Law, a scandal to the priests proud of the Temple, a scandal to his family proud of their respectability, a scandal to the disciples proud of their ambitions.[3]

There is very little resonance here.

SECULAR ATTACK ON RESONANCE

It is plain that secularity has tended to block resonance, and with it faith. A world cut up into pieces, ever smaller and smaller pieces, leading to a pervasive and thoroughgoing atomization, leaves no room for resonance. Indeed, each walled aspect of truth is impervious to all others, fearing them as if they were corruption itself. Each lives by its own authority, autonomously, as if the others did not exist. A kind of acoustical deadness is developed by which faith is deprived of meaning. There are no echoes, no whispers, no overtones in such a world. The great acoustical shells of myth and symbol are anathema. Man's deafness is another word for his alienation.

Yet there are signs that our culture has growth a bit tired of its tiny kingdoms ruled over by dimensional authorities. The body-mind wall has broken down in psychosomatics; the subject-object wall has long since disappeared in philosophy; the individual-community wall has been breached; the fact-symbol wall has disappeared in psychiatry; the art-religion wall no longer holds. Everywhere there are leaks, breaches, break-throughs, and with them a yearning for something better, larger, deeper than kerygmatic mysteries espoused by specialized authority. Moreover, there are other signs which point to a different kind of faith than that of a naïve credulity. It is the much subtler form of faith that identifies the nature of transcendence in precisely a secular world.

In man this capacity to resonate has reached its highest capacity in the will to believe. The hermetically sealed individualist of Ortega, or the reductionist rationalist, or the religious dogmatist,

[3] Samuel H. Miller, *The Life of the Church* (New York: Harper & Bros., 1953), pp. 46 f.

all give up their resonance in the interest of closure. Authority rather than humility becomes the prime virtue of such persons. By restricting the dimension of reality, one can control the issues and speak with absolute finality.

But man is essentially the most permeable of all creatures. In a sense he is infinitely open, available at all levels to all moods of being. He remembers the past and probes the future; he delves deeply and aspires sublimely; all time and space, all history and all possible meanings reverberate in his consciousness. This is the basis of his will to believe, the margin on which faith feeds. Faith and freedom are inextricably related to each other.

Humility is in no sense a derogation of the self; it is basically the recognition that the self is dependent on a vast margin of transcendent reality, in the light of which the individual is indeed small, but not unimportant. Gabriel Marcel draws attention to this criterion of faith in terms of a criticism of our age, when he rebukes it as characterized by its "refusal to reflect, and at the same time the refusal to imagine—for there is a much closer connection between reflecting and imagining than is usually admitted." Or later, as he points out in his use of the words "disponibilité" or "indisponibilité," modern man does not seem to be available, or at hand, for such calls made by life and circumstance. He is neither attentive nor responsive to the flow of happening except in the most cursory manner.[4]

CONTEMPORARY BARRIERS TO RESONANCE

There are three directions in which this resonance of man today has encountered severe barriers in the contemporary secular culture; namely, toward the past, toward transcendence, and toward freedom.

In regard to the past, secularity has developed its own pride and

---

[4] Gabriel Marcel, *The Mystery of Being*, I, *Reflection and Mystery*, G. S. Fraser, trans. (Chicago: Henry Regnery, 1950), p. 36.

rationalized it with considerable historical sophistication. In an epoch when the corridors of time have lengthened backward incredibly, the living memory of our culture grows shorter and shorter. The shocking headlines of yesterday are forgotten in the onslaught of new violences. The memories of our scattered families hold no homestead. Parents and children live in different worlds. Fathers know no skills to teach their astronaut sons. All the arts —architecture, painting, the novel, poetry, drama—tend to "break with the past."

One gets a sense of this pastless present, this traditionless, mobile, fast-moving fugitive in time, the man without roots, in Matteo, the linotyper, who talks about America as contrasted to his native land in Europe, in Harold Rosenberg's book *The Tradition of the New*.

To live over there, one must first forget a few things, also songs. It's a great country, everything's different. You feel it's different, not because of the houses, the skyscrapers, the subways, the elevated. It's different because they never turn to look back, and they don't have anything behind their shoulders. . . . You might just as well forget your real name, it doesn't count for anything. We always have something over our shoulders: the family, the country, the party, our own ideas, and what has happened before, but over there?—Nothing. . . . You must forget everything, throw everything away and always start from the beginning. You must plunge into the water. . . . It's like a revolution that burns up everything that was there before. That's the only way to become an American. You have to enter the circle and run like the rest, hurrying faster and faster. America runs. It's not built like a house that stands firm on its foundations the way we're made. It seems instead like a huge top or a huge gyroscope that rests on the ground on only one fine point and still stays steady because it's whirling, and the faster it whirls the steadier it is. . . . The first colonists had left behind, with no will or chance to return, Europe with its worn parapets and its ancient gods and history. From this voluntary gesture of renunciation was born the new thing that was America. This gesture with all it stood for was the American baptism.[5]

What happens to the resonance of the soul in such a culture? Obviously, the past drops out of sight, drops below the level of attention, drifts away while man is swept along in the furiously pounding, noise-crazed, speed-mad way of life made possible by machines. Take anybody, from peasant to king, a century or more ago, living anywhere in a city or farm, and draw a circle around him large enough to take in everything he would hear about his world on a single day; now take anyone today and try to draw the circle. It would take in the whole world with its tremendous catalogue of catastrophes, revolutions, discoveries, power mowers, deaths. There simply isn't any room left for the past. The present is vast enough, crowded with overwhelming pressures and demands. Our listening is global, not commemorative. Most men look upon the past with condescension. It was not scientific; therefore it must have been quite primitive, meaning below our own times in wisdom. We assume we stand at the pinnacle of the ages, and there is little to be gained by paying attention to the world we have outgrown.

Little wonder then that faith has lost the resonance which could catch the meaning of the great primordial revelations. Careening crazily through space in our power-driven gadgets, it is not likely that we would be in any position to commune with the reflectively inclined images of the Garden of Eden or the crucifix. These occur at a depth in the human center we have long since evacuated. Their truth was not disproved; we have merely moved out of that orbit into a new one, away from the human center into a technical one. We are geniuses in the handling of machines; morons in the handling of life.

How little we seem when we stand up to the great myths and metaphors of the past! The fall of man—like little mice we nibble

[5] New York: Grove Press, 1961, p. 203.

obscenely at the edges of it, reduce it to the crumbly silliness of a complex of ideas, whereas all history is filled with its thunder and no man manages to escape its heart-sickening realities! The suffering servant—like professional technicians we work at a safe distance, behind sterilizing masks, and dissect the whole situation without a single nerve end of our own getting involved in the redemptive agony. The love of God—like broadtailed beavers, we lop the trees and pat down the mud to dam the everlasting waters of mercy where we want them, and dispense them according to our ecclesiastical requirements.

How little can we become? The nonacoustical culture of our time puts us at a disadvantage. It atrophies large dimensions of our life not immediately useful to technology, or reason, or comfort. Turn to any church and see what trouble we have in finding something to do that will really exercise the spirit! What can be done to renew the church? How can we organize a revival? What activities can we schedule which will recover the sense of devotion? Usually we end up building a new wing or adding another minister to the staff; or we start twelve new classes to increase academic information on the Bible; or else we start an endowment just to be on the safe side.

Some time ago I went to see Ingmar Bergman's *Virgin Spring.* It is a cruel, bitter, violent story. A foolish girl, brutal peasants, then rape and death, and finally swift and deliberate vengeance. The powerful reverberations of the tale resound far within the dark recesses of the psyche, awakening deeper and deeper echoes. The soul comes alive at great depths where once only silence and darkness reigned. The resonance of it made ancient classic tragedy a contemporary experience. There were agony and perception which arose from purgation, and pity in the largest sense which arose from perception. One was purged by the burning terror of it, and left without hate, or even bitterness, but only a clean, sharp pity for all who are human.

Probably nothing marks our inadequacy as much in the secular world as precisely the inability to respond to the tragic dimension of existence. As one critic put the matter, "Americans take their tragedy lightly," or, as another said, "Our world has much which is tragic in it, but no tragedy." We lack depth, the resilience of the spirit by which the profound dimensions of suffering are seriously acknowledged. If this be true, it may account more significantly than any other factor for our loss of Christ.

In the second place, we confront a severe acoustical barrier in this horizontal culture in transcendence. In a disenchanted world, fully naturalized, it is hard to find any vestige of transcendence. Anything beyond the natural is out of fashion. Yet in nature the transcendent is either hidden or nonexistent. If it is hidden, then it seems as if we are deceiving ourselves with terms, and we really mean the immanent. Is there any basis for a belief in the transcendent?

Certainly here we have an insight into that predilection of the arts and literature of our day for the brutal contingency of this life. Everything, all the glory and sacrifice, all the sweet esctasy and bitter pain, ends up in the garbage can. Samuel Beckett, Tennessee Williams sift the world down to its dregs and find for the most part simply dregs. Sartre, with superior philosophizing, reduces the human venture to terms of "freedom," "nausea," and "everybody else is hell." Is there any resonance in man for transcendence?

Lionel Trilling characterizes Tolstoi's remarkable perceptiveness in *Anna Karenina* by saying that

> the spirit of man is always at the mercy of the actual and trivial, his passionate sense that the actual and the trivial are of the greatest importance, his certainty that they are not of final importance. Does it not sound like a modest sort of knowledge? Let us not deceive ourselves—*to comprehend unconditioned spirit is not so very hard, but there is no knowledge rarer than the understanding of*

spirit as it exists in the inescapable conditions which the actual and trivial make for it [emphasis is supplied].[6]

This is precisely the problem of identifying the transcendent in the contingent or secular world. This is the burden of resonance.

How far can we catch the reverberation of the spirit in the ordinary, of the sublime in the vulgar? Every great artist and every great saint and prophet has done it. Rembrandt and Hosea, Shakespeare and Isaiah, Dante and Job, found the transcendent not by turning their backs on the drab contingency of the world but by burning through the dross to the eternal.

One of the striking testimonies of the discovery that this most difficult world fits amazingly well the nature of the transcendent is made by G. K. Chesterton in his *Orthodoxy.*

And then followed an experience impossible to describe. It was as if I had been blundering about since my birth with two huge and unmanageable machines, of different shapes and without apparent connection—the world and the Christian tradition. I had found this hole in the world: the fact that one must somehow find a way of loving the world without trusting it; somehow one must love the world without being worldly. I found this projecting feature of Christian theology, like a sort of hard spike, the dogmatic insistence that God was personal, and had made a world separate from Himself. The spike of dogma fitted exactly into the hole in the world— it had evidently been meant to go there—and then the strange thing began to happen. When once these two parts of the two machines had come together, one after another, all the other parts fitted and fell in with an eerie exactitude. I could hear bolt after bolt over all the machinery falling into its place with a kind of click of relief. Having got one part right, all the other parts were repeating that rectitude, as clock after clock strikes noon. Instinct after instinct was answered by doctrine after doctrine. Or, to vary the metaphor, I was like one who had advanced into a hostile country to take one

[6] *The Opposing Self* (New York: The Viking Press, 1955), p. 75. (Italics mine.)

high fortress. And when that fort had fallen the whole country surrendered and turned solid behind me. The whole land was lit up, as it were, back to the first fields of my childhood.[7]

As much as I dislike the mechanical aspect of the metaphor, the experience is unmistakable. And in the process of relating, the contingency of the world, its finite limitations and frustrating refractoriness, are not lost or absorbed or overwhelmed. The world is given another dimension, which both respects its nature—that is to say its secularity—and at the same time redeems it, precisely by adding such a dimension; a dimension, by the way, which is not so much added as revealed.

Let us look, for example, at the birth of Christ as one of the places where this resonance reveals itself. Christmas is not a fiction or a fantasy; it is not idle imagination, embroidering a common tale with uncommonly beautiful but utterly unrealistic legends. It is a story acoustically resonant to the full reverberations of reality. It is sensitive, discerning the implicit dimensions, historical and social, of the birth of a child. It takes a plain event, common and in some respects distressing, and relates it to the sublimest dreams and destinies of the human race.

The incarnation is affirmed in that the ultimate reality is made flesh in a child; the same power that created the world creates this child; the same power that set Adam and Eve in Eden now sets this child in the world. The incarnation, signalized in this child, is the transcendent reality of God present in every finite event. The word becomes flesh—always and everywhere.

Indeed, the way in which the coming of the child resonates to far-off meaning is evident in the doctrine of the Virgin Birth, which has been such a stumbling block for reason. Yet it has remained a persistent element in Western tradition. Is it not possible that this

---

[7] G. K. Chesterton, *Orthodoxy* (New York: Dodd, Mead & Company, 1936), pp. 127 f., quoted in Joseph Sittler, *The Ecology of Faith* (Philadelphia: Muhlenberg Press, 1961), p. 43.

elucidates the fact that the person Jesus the Christ cannot be explained by his biological antecedents, his father or his mother; that the mystery in him transcends the causal sequences of our human life; in short, that he is more intimately related to God than he is to his own father and mother? This surely becomes revealing, not by restricting it to Jesus, but by acknowledging the actuality in the phrase that all men are God's children. We are all more intimately bound up with God; He is more the determiner of our being than our father in the flesh.

This kind of resonance would make a great deal more sense of the figure of Jesus were it allowed to be held up to the realities of man and history. In him there are such magnitudes of being that the height and depth, the length and breadth of man are embraced. He is the Word and the World; and he holds both together; he is truth and suffering, life and death, goodness and scandal, judgment and compassion. In him the relationship of God and contingency is illumined; in him the tension between power and love, between conscience and forgiveness, between justice and mercy, between prayer and history burns to a white heat. His name reverberates in our hearts, our lives in his life, because deep speaketh unto deep, and unless we are stone-deaf the profoundest magnitudes of our being respond to his "victory of faith" in which he overcame the world by his perceptive love of it.

One of the frustrations any modern mind is likely to have with tradition is the "closed Christ." He has become the idol of many theological systems, and by making a quick flourish in the name of indisputable orthodoxy every attempt to reach Christ by a human path is taken away. The sacrosanct formula is Christocentric; indeed, there is much to make one believe that certain systems have become Christocentric at the expense of God. This I take to be idolatrous and basically un-Christian. A Christ whose validity is enclosed, whose nature is sealed off from all real contamination by the world, the flesh, and the devil—in short, with any intrinsic involvement in concrete history—is as superfluous, irrelevant, and worthless as a God totally separated from the world. To be of worth, Christ must be open on all sides; indeed, he is openness, manifesting the aspect of freedom in participation, and transcendence in humility, whereby history is reconciled to God and life in this world becomes eternal. He is open, the prime resonance in whom all things reverberate and by whom the music of God's praise rises even from the cross.

That exploration of Christology which does not illumine the nature of our striving to be reconciled to God is no Christology at all, but a game. Christ is the prospect par excellence of the secular, he was the Word made flesh; in a sense, he discovered the world, denied its wonders and refused its magic, suffered its hate and healed it of insanity. There is a truth in that he came from God and faced the world, lived in it and through it to the bitterest death and shame, and yet made plain that God was not absent.

Resonance for the past is one thing; resonance for the transcendent in the present another; but what can we say about resonance within the man himself? It seems to me this is the place where, if there is to be any meaning in freedom or in the future or in grace, it must occur. Freedom is that openness which constitutes the reality of the spirit; though man's body is enmeshed in the net of casual sequences, he rises far beyond time and the limitations of space, and by insight, imagination, and will he transforms the world all along the dimension of his inner freedom. In a sense, this is his future, the earnest of his own transcendence, the yet-to-be for which he dies willingly to the old.

And somewhere in this same dimension of freedom, of spirit, of openness, of *disponibilité*, we discover grace. In a sense, it is the reverberation itself. The whole creation shouts from a thousand sides, from every level, in all things and events—shouts and presses forward, pouring into every available opening to lift and fill, as a tide with the strength of the whole earth and its planets pours with undeniable power into every creek and cove.

Rilke speaks of this:

> Even today . . . existence is magical, pouring
> freshly from hundreds of well springs—a playing of purest
> forces, which none can surprise without humbly adoring.
> Words still melt into something beyond their embrace
> Music too keeps building anew with the insecurest
>   stones her celestial house in unused space.[8]

So it is that the dying priest in Bernanos' *Diary of a Country Priest* comes at last to say, "Grace is everywhere." Obviously, this does not make sense unless one has moved into perspective and can stand where he stood. But a world where faith keeps the life of man open and resonant to the larger realities, open to the past and to the transcendent—even a secular world is then not without grace, simply because grace comes to such a world whenever man reconciles it to God, as Christ did. The secular world is merely the waiting world, the world waiting for its full meaning. We may deny it, betray it, ruin it; but if we have faith, if we have room enough in ourselves to be resonant, then it may become as religious as any world man has ever known.

---

[8] Rainer Maria Rilke, *Sonnets to Orpheus* (New York: W. W. Norton & Co., 1942), Part 2, Sonnet 10.

(6) The Perplexity and Passion of the Preacher

There is an unforgettable portrait of a minister in *The Notebooks of Malte Laurids Brigge,* by Rainer Maria Rilke. He says:

> All at once it had got to the point again when the minister, Dr. Jesperson, had to be invited. Accustomed to a very pious neighborhood which always went into dissolution on his account, Dr. Jesperson was entirely out of his element with us; he was, so to speak, lying on dry land and gasping. The gills he had developed for himself worked with difficulty; bubbles formed and the whole thing was not without its danger. Of material for conversation there was to be exactly none whatever; remainders were being disposed of at unbelievable prices, it was a liquidation of all stocks. In our house Dr. Jesperson had to content himself with being a private person; but that was exactly what he had never been. As far back as he could think, his profession had been the soul. For him the soul was a

public institution which he represented, and he saw to it that he was never off duty, not even in his relations with his wife.[1]

The image is finely focused by the author's grandmother, whose sense of reality was shocked by this ecclesiastical mannequin. "However can he drive about," she sometimes said, "and go in to see people, just when they are dying."

This is the question: how can the minister be real just when life deepens down to its ultimate realities, its final mysteries? How can he retain the integrity of a private person and yet not eschew his religious office? Indeed, nothing is so much in jeopardy today as the integrity of the minister. There is a widespread doubt that the Sunday habit of the minister, his talk, his sermonic air, his moralistic finickiness, his always-proper guise, is anything but a thin fake. The attempt to reduce the Sunday habit to something indubitably real, by jests, informal casualness, clever virtuosity, or even snide vulgarity, is a temptation which does not improve the situation.

How can we be God's men and not fall prey on the one hand to a smooth but vacuous mouthing of traditional clichés and pious patter, or on the other hand to the equally thin but sophisticated gospels of popularized science or glib generalities of Freudian habits? To stand firmly in the religious realm and just as firmly in the twentieth century, to speak profoundly of faith and to make it cogent in an age of secularity is our primary task, and no amount of hiding one half from the other half will suffice.

Integrity in the minister cannot be purchased any less cheaply than in any other calling. As James Baldwin, the novelist, puts it:

In my mind, the effort to become a great novelist simply involves attempting to tell as much of the truth as one can bear, and then a little more. It is an effort which, by its very nature—remembering that men write the books, that time passes and energy flags, and

[1] New York: W. W. Norton & Co., 1949, p. 96.

safety beckons—is obviously doomed to failure. Success is an American word which cannot conceivably, unless it is defined in an extremely severe, ironical and painful way, have any place in the vocabulary of any artist. . . . The air of this time and place is so heavy with rhetoric, so thick with soothing lies, that one must do great violence to language, one must somehow disrupt the comforting beat in order to be heard. Obviously one must dismiss any hopes one may have ever had of winning a popularity contest.[2]

PERPLEXITY AND PASSION

In the real ministry there will be both perplexity and passion. The classic molds have been broken, and the new way is not yet marked out. There will be plenty of perplexity if a man strives to be honest, to himself, to God, and to his people. And in that honesty there will be passion, passion in the sense of suffering, suffering at every level, sometimes economically, or socially, or intellectually, or spiritually. An honest man, and I assume this is the first and most difficult achievement as well as the rarest—an honest man will be often perplexed and often in passion.

By perplexity I mean standing in a world where all the signposts are down and the language has changed, and nobody knows where the sun is going to rise; a world where the clocks are all telling a different time and everybody is late and going nowhere in a hurry; where everybody dreads the future, has no time for the past, and wears a mask in order to see as little as possible of the present.

By passion I mean taking hold of the world where it is most mysterious, where it has no shape and shows no meaning; I mean lifting old stories and bearing their weight, putting the heart under old sorrows until its dry, cracked earth feels the tears that men have wept; I mean remembering the deep, deep well into which a child looked, and in the terror or ecstasy saw eternity and could never forget it and was forever lonely afterward; I mean holding in both hands the sweet, terrible gifts of love and trust, and know-

[2] *New York Times Book Review,* January 14, 1962, Section 7, Part 1, pp. 1, 38.

ing how poor and cheap and twisted one's heart has been, turned and tangled by its silly vanity and the swaggering bluff of pride.

By perplexity I mean to quit all mumbo jumbo, to look life in the face, to shut one's mouth in silence and let the weight of the world come down upon the tender tissue of the heart till it bursts and bruises and one cannot tickle the tongue any longer with the sweet honey of sanctimonious prattle.

By passion I mean suffering, no different from any other man's, brought out into the center of life, uncovered before God, the suffering of one's own shame and sin and self, the suffering of loving the good but doing the evil, of wanting more light but crawling comfortably into the dark, of reaching for God but being desperately afraid of finding Him.

By perplexity I mean standing with Adam when he reaches into the tree of the knowledge of good and evil; with Jacob when, wrestling with the nameless angel, he feels the searing twinge of his hip breaking; with Hosea when he feels like a fool loving one who scarcely seems worth it; with Isaiah when he glimpses the strange glory of utter failure in the suffering servant; with Jesus, who went beyond the sure comfort of God.

By passion I mean suffering the inexplicable grace of God, given in the most unexpected places under impossible conditions, for seemingly no reason at all; in mercy that tormented and joy that haunted, in love that followed fleeing footsteps and in peace that stilled the anger and tumult of a hot heart.

In an age of secularity, the role of the minister is, to say the least, problematical. To what exactly in such a world does he address himself? In an age which has lost all vestiges of unity and sanctity, how does he speak of God? In the midst of surplus and plenty, what will he say of asceticism or even discipline? With the compulsive activism of a fluid society and an extraverted culture, how will he commend any of the contemplative arts or skills of worship or prayer? In a time which does not stand still long enough to establish a center, how will he make something out of the church? With literalists on every hand, intent on making the plain fact as prosaic as possible, what kind of strategy can he use to justify myth or sacrament? With the state providing security, and the psychiatrists pastoral care, and education the initiation into society, what is left to say for salvation, or redemption, or conversion? Other than keeping respectability intact, or solemnizing marriages, or maintaining a heavy suggestion of otherworldliness at funerals, what can a minister do?

A CONFUSING ROLE

There is no doubt that in general the minister feels perplexed about his role. Otherwise it would be hard to understand the way in which he has run hither and yon in the effort to rehabilitate it both in his own and in the public eye. He has made it over in terms of more acceptable guises. He has hit upon the smooth executive type in a time when churches have become big institutions in need of management. Large congregations, big plants, large budgets—all have conspired to transform the man of God into a big operator. It is true that he loses for the most part the abilities of priest or prophet in the process, but even so the "church" thrives. Or else he finds that there are a great many people physically in the twentieth century but mentally, culturally, still living in the nineteenth, or earlier. He can still talk the language of a previous age with solemn assurance in the conservative precincts of the church and build the unwindowed walls that stand imperviously between the Sunday ethos and the workday routine. Or he may take off in the opposite direction, jettisoning Christ, Bible, tradition, everything earlier than his own entrance upon the human scene, and announce himself as a "free mind."

If he clings tenaciously to the traditional image, he is likely to find himself literally outside the life of his people; if he identifies himself with the life of the time, he is likely to find himself outside the realm of anything substantially religious.

Not long ago, an enterprising and not unphilosophical photographer published a book of fascinating candid camera shots of famous people caught in mid-air while they were jumping. The artist-photographer had a serious intention, not at all humorous, which he formulated in brief descriptions interpreting the mental attitudes of actors, bankers, theologians, from Brigitte Bardot to Paul Tillich, using their peculiar expression in mid-air as evidence. The more I reflected on the phenomenon, the less I thought of individuals and the more of the act itself. Indeed, in the current search for symbols, I felt I had found one. It looked to me as if the picture of a man caught in mid-air might well be a proper symbol for the contemporary minister. After all, he is up in the air and no one knows quite where he is going to land, not even the minister himself. If any profession has grown confused about itself, its role in the world, it is the ministry. There was a time when the structures of confidence in our culture were religious, and the minister stood on solid ground. Today the structures of confidence are not religious but scientific or social or even commercial, and in this culture the minister has mighty little ground, if any, to stand on. He is caught in an agony of tense confusion, halfway between a world that has largely disappeared and a new world that has not yet found a place for him.

Any man unaware of this pervading ambiguity, this appalling suspension in mid-air, this being like a fish out of water, simply fails to observe the first condition he must somehow transcend. One cannot be blind to the fact that by being a minister one is separated from men and women with whom Christ would have shared his bread and his talk; the hard and clanking coat of mail with which respectability clothes the preacher hides him as a human being; the sheltering proprieties of moralistic congregations build as thick a wall between the minister and the world as any medieval monastery ever did for the cloistered monk.

There must be an authentic base for the Christian ministry even in a secular world. Its very authenticity may be epitomized by perplexity. After all, is this not the perennial tension between faith and the world, and is not our situation all the more sharply defined? The world stands out today unmistakably itself, clean and dry, so to speak, not blurred by transcendent mirages of any kind; and over against it the question of faith, of meaning, of God, and of man's destiny.

The usual assumption that it would be an easier world for faith were the contrast less definite, or were the circumstances less threatening, or were the dire consequences of our actions less evident, is scarcely to be trusted. When all things make for faith, it is scarcely faith that results. We stand at a juncture of history when much of the fog, whether of vague romanticism or ecclesiastical superstition, has rolled back from the world and left it exposed. It surely has been many generations since we have seen it so clearly, so plainly for what it is. On every hand it challenges the response of man to do what he will with it. The question of what function faith bears in such a time is asked as much by the world as it is by the church. Indeed, it may be that by virtue of the world made plain we may begin to see more clearly what faith can be.

Not long ago Charles Malik spoke eloquently of what can be called the favorable aspect of this uneasy and precarious time.

> Life then was too smooth, too placid, in a sense too innocent; therefore, there was no need to penetrate beneath the surface. You could live a lifetime then without having to ask a fundamental question or face a fundamental issue. But today he must be a dead man or a thoroughly corrupt man who is not forced into depths. And the more we go into the depths of the spirit, the more we understand the gospel and the more we feel that every word in it, every turn of thought in it, every little incident in it, illuminates the depths and puts us in touch with the creative power of God.[3]

THE SECULAR CHURCH

How can we pick up this "perplexity and passion" as ministers? Where can we pry the problem loose and find places to work on

[3] Charles Malik, "The Gospel and the Life of the Spirit," *The Christian Century*, August 23, 1961, p. 1,000.

it? Let us begin by saying frankly that the first problem of the minister is the secularized church. This may sound strange when the recurring refrain of these chapters, the church's unreality, is remembered. Yet it is precisely the unreality of the church that is symptomatic of its secularization. If men are saying at work, "What sense is there to all this frenzy, the vast push for more and more, the maggotlike crawling of interminable mobility, changing policies, new packaging, mergers and discontinuance, scrambling up and down the ladder, being kind for three days to the VIP until the order is snagged?"—what if all this is transported into the church, learned, and then labeled with terms like "evangelism," "a live church," "brotherly love," "sacrificial giving," and so on? The natural reaction is simply nausea, and quite properly so.

The minister finds himself in a nasty jam. Unless he plays the game, promotes success, snags new members in exciting numbers, keeps the program humping, stirs the air with the flash of bright inspirations, opens up new resources and new markets, oils the works with suavity and poise, plays the impresario with all the organizations, increases the congregation and ups the budget— then by every rule of thumb in current use his name is mud, not only as far as the local church is concerned, but as well with the bureaucracy that controls the next step up the ladder on the basis of the record.

Indeed, a man is not a minister very long before he discovers that the local church is a unique kind of world. It has its own kind of building, its own kind of language, its own inner hierarchy, its own law, its own ethos, its own unwritten code, its own self-justification, its own notion of tradition, its own version of authority. None of these things may have more than accidental reference to the classical Christian ethos or biblical mores. In the light of them, the minister might well ask, "How much 'reality intake' can this church stand before it ousts me as a disturber of the peace? How honest can it become in facing the world it avers it wants to save? How bold will it be in confronting the agony and anguish the world is suffering? How humbly will it acknowledge its poverty, and how generously will it recognize the grace of God in uncclesiastical settings and in unrighteous people? Is it anything more than a soft cocoon spun out of our all-too-human weakness as a buffer against the uncomfortable tensions and necessities of the real world, and is there any way to introduce the rigor of the gospel to such infantile dependents? What can be done to bring the church back into the circle where the flash of wings can be seen and the contest is real in the heart of man to find the name of the mystery with which he wrestles in the darkness?"

FOUR DIRECTIONS FOR THE MINISTRY

For the minister himself, there stands an endless discipline by which he may work out his salvation. There are four directions in which the minister may serve God without losing his soul or his integrity—four ways which stand a man precisely in the midst of the secular world to express his faith vis-à-vis the conditions it establishes for all of us. He should resume connections with humanity; transcend technical and urban shrewdness; transmute the indigenous confession of circumstance by the power of the spirit; and, finally, recover such arts and skills as to celebrate worship powerfully enough to reveal God, resurrect man, and redeem society.

Impossible? Of course it is impossible. You are right! It is far beyond us. There is no chance of reaching it. It is incredible! Imagine—that last phrase—reveal God, resurrect man, and redeem society. . . . Any man is a fool to think it can be done. What nonsense! And yet, we should ponder this. It may be our job. If it is a fool's job, then we can either resign or stay with it. The question is, can we stay with it? Can we stay with it faithfully, honestly, stubbornly?

Let us pick up the four points, impossible as they are, one by one. The first declares that the minister should resume connection with humanity. For a minister to get separated from the real life of this world is, in the final analysis, to be separated from God. To speak and act as if he were a privileged character, free of any complicity in the world as such, pure of its sullied and embarrassing strife, far beyond its rebellious doubt or its sickening despair, divinely appointed, as it were, because of a mysterious, superior status to be a kind of official in the grand manner, a sort of deputy forever polishing the badges of his impeccable role—this is downright shameful.

But the truth is, such docetism, hollowness, unreality is widespread for two reasons. It is easy to wrap oneself up in a vocabulary, traditionally sacrosanct and socially beyond criticism, layer on layer, year after year, until the mumification is complete. There is no life within, but the sarcophagus is embellished with all the golden words and mellifluous diction of Scripture and sanctuary. It is easy because it is safe; it requires no thinking; and the chameleonlike camouflage is a source of both self-satisfaction and obvious gratification of fulfilling the desire and expectation of so many others.

The second reason for the widespread existential vacuum in the ministry is that it is hard to keep in contact with reality. Reality is simply not easy to bear; we cannot stand it for very long; we find all kinds of exits and escapes; we come up for air very quickly; we do everything we can to create distractions. It takes a saint to stay at the level of reality; few of us are so gifted. This perennial and persistent problem is as old as history, as old as the wavering, uncertain consciousness of man that flutters like a candle in the winds of time.

But it is also a special and difficult ordeal for a minister. He is tempted to live in the church, for the church, molded by its special language, habituated to its routine, domesticated by its specious securities, corrupted by its prudent mendacity. In a secular age, religion is expurgated from the rest of the world—from work, from the home, from holidays—and put into one place, the church. There it is enacted with special words and special ideas and special feelings. Such unnatural concentration creates an artificial situation in which religion tends to be concerned with being religious. It poses and gestures in its own mirror. It has nothing but itself to work with; it is like trying to embroider embroidery, or to paint pigment. Essentially it is spiritual incest. The proper object of religion is the world.

As Martin Buber explains:

> Only he who believes in the world is given power to enter into dealings with it, and if he gives himself to this he cannot remain godless. If only we love the real world, that will not let itself be extinguished, really in its horror, if only we venture to surround it with the arms of our spirit, our hands will meet hands that grip them.
>
> I know nothing of a "world" and a "life in the world" that might separate a man from God. What is thus described is actually life with an alienated world.[4]

But let us press the matter further. It is hard to keep your eye on this world; to keep it in focus, so to speak. It slides away from us quickly; we make it over in our eyes till we see what we want to see and remain blind to what we dislike. We screen it in our minds until we keep what we want and drop far into limbo what we wish were not there.

Few of us live in this age, or at least we live only partly in this age. Some of us are paleolithic in art, iron age in politics, Victorian in morals, and only modern in the gadgets and plumbing we love and the cars we drive. There is some difficulty in moving entirely into the twentieth century. We love so much that is no longer true of the world that we cannot bear to give up the fiction.

There is no need for me to enumerate the spurious gospels running rampant in America, which not only distort reality but dream up a lie about life, back it with God's name, and sell it to fools whose hearts are aching for a special place in heaven which will

---

[4] Martin Buber, *I and Thou*, Ronald Gregor Smith, trans. (Edinburgh: T. & T. Clark, 1937), pp. 94 f.

cost them nothing. The sad thing is that Flopsy Mopsy Cottontail versions of the New Testament can be passed off as the message of the crucified Lord. It is a world full of exits, softly padded and patrolled by priests of all faiths who lavishly dispense the divine patronage.

In the face of this, one is brought to his senses by the cold dash of those men and women who are wrestling with the reality of our time. They bear the marks of the encounter, as did Jacob and Jesus, for they are not blindfolded nor do they fight with padded gloves. The iron of this world has entered into their souls. Their stigmata have come from bearing the burden of our age.

I think of the profound torment of Kafka, in whose heart the shadows cast by God's absence were like a glory that both damned and glorified him; I think of Simone Weil, whose vicarious suffering for her fellows kept her from ever joining the church; I think of Camus, whose clear and honest sight shamed us all, who named in courage the absurdity we all must live with and die with, and who called on all of us to be done with the bloated compassion which is institutionally produced, by which we actually aimlessly assume the suffering of our brothers all over the world. Time would fail me to tell of others, but the world is full of their voices and their acts are witnessing to a new visitation, a new revelation outside the courts of the temple.

Our task is to see this age, the pain and apostasy of it, and to see it clearly, to keep our eye on it until we see what is in it and what it means. We need scholars to tell us about Greece and Rome, the Bible and the Reformation, but we also need men to tell us about this world, this new world full of forces and fantasies, of guilt and glory, of wealth and woe, of machines and misery, of dread and dreams, of space travel and suicidal despair. There is a furious jumble here, a mighty burgeoning of power, a march of madness and millions of men, a lust for power and a huge concern for health and freedom. And at the center of it is man himself—turned, twisted, tormented, pummeled, lured and thrust, shaken and striving, sickened and bragging, satiated and starved, scarred and star-bent, wounded, puzzled, sure of himself, baffled and lonely and withal unspent.

What do you and I—living in this age as much as we can, as much as we have the courage and humility to—what do we make of it? Secular, disenchanted, naturalized, with all the magic removed, with revelation back there a long time ago and removed from us, with God nostalgically remembered but no longer employed; with thundering machines to set our tempo, and silent boxes of tubes to settle our problems; with families crumbling and cities growing like great tumors, and vast states restless in the grip of political paranoia.

We must look at this age as intently as the dramatist or the poet or the novelist. We dare not be any less attentive than the scientist. We must listen and learn as carefully and as concernedly as the psychiatrist. If we do this, we may not talk as much, but what we say may mean something to those who are carrying the weight of the world on their bewildered hearts.

Nor need we go far to listen to the voices of this age. There are Dostoevski and Kierkegaard and Nietzsche—don't tell me they lived a hundred years ago! They are still in the future for most of us; they know a great deal into which we have yet to be born. And there are Beckett and Arthur Miller and William Faulkner and Lagerkvist and Kafka and Ionesco and Sartre. Not all to our liking, to be sure, but voices that have one thing in common. They are shouting from the center of man's lonely and beleaguered heart, uttering *de profundis* what it means to be human in an age like this, confronted by a startling and unmistakable vision of its raw contingency, without having within easy reach the ancient and well-remembered mercy of a God who no longer seems to be here.

Now the second way opens for the minister to retain his integrity in a secular age, by transcending its *shrewdness*. I use the word in a large and generic sense to cover the kind of sophisticated illusion that essentially human problems are no different from any other, and can be solved by intellectual or even technical means. This age is singularly confident in its use of techniques, organization, research, and measurement, subtle or otherwise, to eliminate the troubles "of our angry dust."

Any thoroughgoing reflection on this reveals quickly that man is thus relieved of any essential responsibility for his own life or destiny. He is dislocated from the center, and his freedom—which is to say, his responsibility—is betrayed. Nowhere does this become plainer than in the way man has come to treat of himself as a totally conditioned creature whose responsibility is near the zero mark. He thus becomes one more item in a complicated system of action and reaction, and his task is merely to adjust himself to the flotsam and jetsam of his days as comfortably and with as little anxiety as possible.

There are, however, many levels of reality both beyond and below the horizontal sophistication of our age. Our sensibility at such levels may be clumsy, unresponsive, or even atrophied, but it can be recovered, and the vitality of a larger consciousness can be elicited by attention and witness. T. S. Eliot reminds us in writing of Dante that Shakespeare understands a greater extent and variety of human life than Dante; but that Dante understands "deeper degrees of degradation and higher degrees of exaltation." Later in the same essay he says, "It took me many years to recognize that the states of improvement and beatitude which Dante describes are still further from what the modern world can conceive as cheerfulness than are his states of damnation. . . . Nowhere in poetry has experience so remote from ordinary experience been expressed so concretely."[5]

Indeed, what I am pleading for at this juncture is the recovery or resurrection of those capacities of our humanity too long smothered or neglected by the excessive attention we have given to industrial or technical matters. Our power over nature has increased

[5] T. S. Eliot, *Selected Essays, 1917–1932* (New York: Harcourt, Brace & Co., 1932), pp. 214, 223, 227.

incredibly, while the scope of our inner sensibility has shrunken alarmingly. We simply have little resonance left in us to respond to the mighty ranges of the spirit which were commonly known to ordinary men in biblical times. The opening up of these heights and depths, the careful description of the scope of human sensibility, the exploration of these higher and lower registers of reality —this is our work as ministers if we are to conserve the full magnitude of our humanity in an age when many forces and factors conspire toward its attrition.

The third path of integrity lies in the transmuting of the indigenous confusion of circumstance by the spirit. If we began with the reassertion of the specifically human reality as over against abstractions, then transcended the shrewdness of the technical and urban methods of dealing with reality, we come now to the power of our humanity to transmute the contradictions and confusions of our experience into such unity as inheres in beauty or faith or goodness. Put in its classical religious terminology, this is the redemptive power of the spirit and needs to be reaffirmed as over against the shrewdness of secularity. By it, secularity is saved from its meaninglessness, its impersonality, its lostness, its incompleteness.

Traditionally, the power of God has been conceived as coming directly to the world, detouring around man, and changing the world in order to adjust it to man's higher hopes and desires. This is scarcely what we have seen when our eyes have been open. God's power has moved through that level of man's self we call the spirit, through the power of his freedom and faith, and thus transmuted the world, bringing it into unity and significance. In Paul's word, "the whole creation has been groaning in travail together" and "waits with eager longing for the revealing of the sons of God." When they are manifest, then creation is fulfilled. God's grace reasserts the human center.

This is the highest moral power open to man. By it he embraces the manifold diversity of life and experience and by the spirit manages to bring it into such a transformed condition that "all things work together for good." Night and day, joy and sorrow, life and death, faith and reason, infancy and age, man and woman —all things are seen steadily, boldly, and whole. Nothing is omitted. The word and the flesh, God and the world, time and eternity, man and the devil—the tremendous stretches by which our lives are tormented are to be transmuted by faith. This arduous exercise of the spirit is well illustrated by a letter of Keats in which he describes the genius of Shakespeare as "burning through the evil." A great poet, he says, looks at human life, sees the terrible truth of its evil, but sees it so intensely that it becomes an element of the beauty that is created in the act of perception. Our task is nothing less than to lift the whole mass of human experience, not subtracting the portions we dislike, and by the labor of our imagination shape it to fit our soul's highest needs.

Possibly one of the secrets of this transmutation is the hint we gather from the work of the saints. Lavelle describes their particular genius as their ability to "lend inwardness to whatever event they meet." It is in such inwardness that the leverage is afforded by which the world is transformed and its life redeemed. As Lavelle continues:

> It is this miracle which the saint continually reveals to us: a miracle in which every thing, while still retaining its own identity, suddenly displays an essence and significance which otherwise would have eluded us. The intelligence is thus restored to its proper sphere of activity. It is not true to say that the saint has turned his back on the world. On the contrary, he is the only one who has access to the deep life of the world, instead of remaining merely on the surface. Far from vanishing like a dream, the world reveals to him the deep foundations on which it rests.[6]

The fourth and last of these roles in which the minister may operate with integrity is that of celebrant. I use the word celebrant

[6] Louis Lavelle, *The Meaning of Holiness*, Dorothea Sullivan, trans. (London: Burns & Oates, 1954), pp. 13, 27.

deliberately. A minister should know how to celebrate. In the midst of this age, in the maelstrom of history in all its fury, in the muddled mess of this world, in the confusion and boredom and amazement, he ought to be able to spot something—an event, a person, a memory, an act, a turning of the soul, the flash of bright wings, the surprise of sweet compassion—somewhere he ought to be able to pick out a glory to celebrate. There should be something somewhere hidden in the common day, muffled by the plain speech of a plain man, to break the sky asunder, to ascend on high in song.

What this simple and glorious word "to celebrate" means is that the minister must recover such arts and skills as to act in worship with the power to reveal God, to resurrect man, and to redeem the world. This is indeed a large order, especially when it is remembered that most of the arts and skills that lie behind the exercise of contemplation have either evaporated in the heat of activism or have been vulgarized by the circus of contemporary mass media. As for revealing God by an act of worship, what does this mean? Or in resurrecting man, do we mean that he has suffered death? Or in redeeming society, do we mean it has undergone a perversion in the secular age? And, if so, how does the act of worship help?

If worship is anything at all, it is an act by which we reaffirm an image of reality derived from historic events by which our confidence in God is sustained. The image of reality may be in the highest degree paradoxical; indeed, it would not suffice were the most awful contradictions omitted. It is a visual articulation of that mystery by which God is revealed under the very conditions which seem to deny Him. This is an epiphany, not in glory but in the terms of this world, elevated as witness and re-enacted as hope, that nowhere can God be denied and the world adequately adumbrated. By this act, God is revealed in the world where He seems to be absent.

Moreover, by it man is resurrected. By attrition he dies a thousand deaths, retreats by endless betrayals to lower levels, repudiates himself for the comfort of forgetting his own reality, and yet his very flight and guilt carry symptoms of a hunger that he cannot stifle. In the act of worship, in the presence of the ineluctable humanity, in the upper and nether depths of the divine contradiction, between life and death, his own image is unmistakable. He worships by re-enacting his own mystery of becoming; he worships only when he is born again, resurrected from the dead.

And finally, in the act of worship society is redeemed. There are no chains so cruel as those which bind men to men in community. Ignorance and malice aggravate every human tie. Only where these can be openly illumined by the common acknowledgment of sin and lifted to the assurance of divine mercy, can society be relieved of its burden of guilt and its harrowing hate. In the act of worship, in the figure of the crucified, image of reality and sign of the resurrected, society itself is transmuted and becomes the fellowship of saints, not because of its perfection but because of its compassion.

Index

(*111*)